Microsoft® Word 2002 Manual for

GREGG

College Keyboarding & Document Processing

**9th Edition
Lessons 1-120**

Ober
Johnson
Rice
Hanson

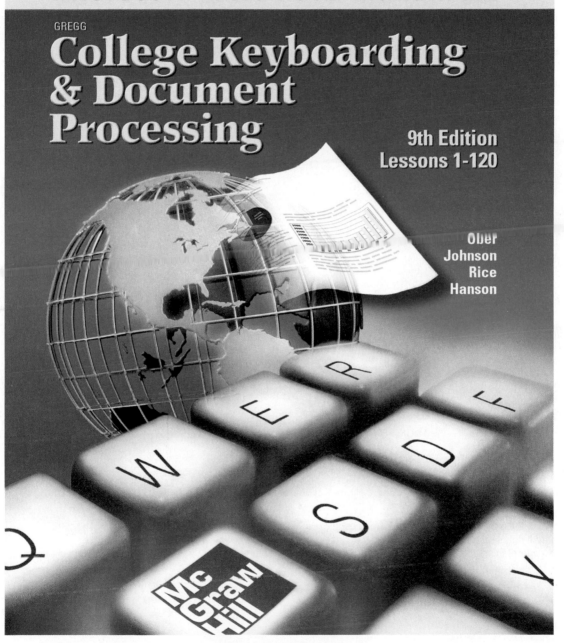

**Glencoe
McGraw-Hill**

New York, New York   Columbus, Ohio   Chicago, Illinois   Peoria, Illinois   Woodland Hills, California

Notes to user: Your screens may not be identical to the illustrations shown in this book. The dynamic capabilities of Word 2002 result in toolbars and/or keystrokes that change as options are used.

The toolbars show only buttons used most recently; many other buttons are available. To look for a button not shown on the docked toolbars, click the More Buttons button at the end of the toolbars. When a button is used that is not displayed on the toolbars, Word moves that button to the docked toolbars.

Glencoe/McGraw-Hill

A Division of The **McGraw·Hill** *Companies*

Microsoft is a registered trademark, and Windows is a trademark, of Microsoft Corporation.

Microsoft® Word 2002 Manual for Gregg College Keyboarding & Document Processing™ 9th Edition

Send all inquiries to:
Glencoe/McGraw-Hill
21600 Oxnard Street, Suite 500
Woodland Hills, CA 91367-4947

Printed in the United States of America.

ISBN: 0-07-830386-9

3 4 5 6 7 8 9   071   06 05 04 03 02

Contents

Reference Manual

Getting Started

Reference Manual

A. MAJOR PARTS OF A MICROCOMPUTER SYSTEM

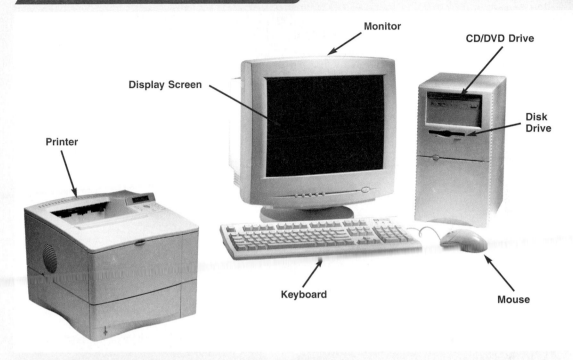

Monitor

CD/DVD Drive

Display Screen

Disk Drive

Printer

Keyboard

Mouse

B. THE COMPUTER KEYBOARD

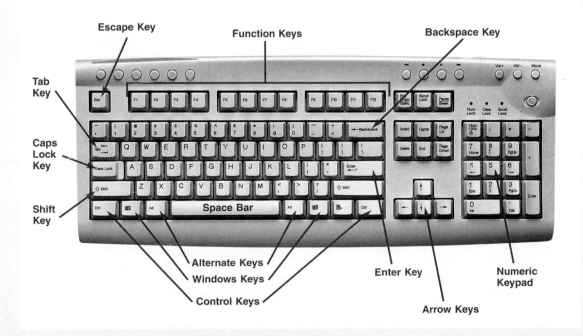

Escape Key

Function Keys

Backspace Key

Tab Key

Caps Lock Key

Shift Key

Alternate Keys

Windows Keys

Control Keys

Enter Key

Arrow Keys

Numeric Keypad

Reference Manual

A. BUSINESS LETTER
(in block style with standard punctuation)

Letterhead	**NATIONAL GEOGRAPHIC SOCIETY**

↓6X

Date line   September 5, 20-- ↓4X

Inside address   Ms. Joan R. Hunter
Bolwater Associates
One Parklands Drive
Darien, CT 06820 ↓2X

Salutation   Dear Ms. Hunter: ↓2X

Body   You will soon receive the signed contract to have your organization conduct a one-day workshop for our employees on eliminating repetitive-motion injuries in the workplace. As we agreed, this workshop will apply to both our office and factory workers and you will conduct separate sessions for each group.

We revised Paragraph 4b to require the instructor of this workshop to be a full-time employee of Bolwater Associates. In addition, we made changes to Paragraph 10-c to require our prior approval of the agenda for the workshop.

If these revisions are satisfactory, please sign and return one copy of the contract for our files. We look forward to this opportunity to enhance the health of our employees. I know that all of us will enjoy this workshop. ↓2X

Complimentary closing   Sincerely, ↓4X

John L. Merritt

Writer's identification   John L. Merritt, Director ↓2X

Reference initials   fej

1145 17th Street N.W., Washington, D.C. 20036-4688, U.S.A.   Telephone: (202) 857-7537   Fax: (202) 429-5776
♻ Recycled-content paper

B. BUSINESS LETTER IN MODIFIED-BLOCK STYLE
(with open punctuation, multiline list, and enclosure notation)

8787 Orion Place
Columbus, OH 43240-4027
Tel 614 430 6000
Fax 614 430 6621

SRA/McGraw-Hill
A Division of The McGraw-Hill Companies

↓6X
→tab to centerpoint   May 15, 20-- ↓4X

Ms. Joan R. Hunter
Bolwater Associates
One Parklands Drive
Darien, CT 06820 ↓2X

Dear Ms. Hunter ↓2X

I am returning a signed contract to have your organization conduct a one-day workshop for our employees on eliminating repetitive-motion injuries in the workplace. We have made the following changes to the contract:

Multiline list   1.   We revised Paragraph 4b to require the instructor of this workshop to be a full-time employee of Bolwater Associates.

2.   We made changes to Paragraph 10-c to require our prior approval of the agenda for the workshop.

If these revisions are satisfactory, please sign and return one copy of the contract for our files. We look forward to this opportunity to enhance the health of our employees. I know that all of us will enjoy this workshop. ↓2X

→tab to centerpoint   Sincerely, ↓4X

John L. Merritt

John L. Merritt, Director ↓2X

pec

Enclosure notation   Enclosure

C. BUSINESS LETTER IN SIMPLIFIED STYLE
(with single-line list, enclosure notation, and copy notation)

20 Ryan Ranch Road
Monterey, CA 93940
Tel 831 393 7900
800 538 9547 ext. 7900
Fax 831 393 7211

CTB/McGraw-Hill
A Division of The McGraw-Hill Companies

↓6X

October 5, 20-- ↓4X

Ms. Joan R. Hunter
Bolwater Associates
One Parklands Drive
Darien, CT 06820 ↓3X

WORKSHOP CONTRACT ↓3X

I am returning the signed contract, Ms. Hunter, to have your organization conduct a one-day workshop for our employees on eliminating repetitive-motion injuries in the workplace. We have amended the following sections of the contract:

Single-line list   •   Paragraph 4b
•   Table 3
•   Attachment 2

If these revisions are satisfactory, please sign and return one copy of the contract for our files. We look forward to this opportunity to enhance the health of our employees. I know that all of us will enjoy this workshop. ↓4X

John L. Merritt

JOHN L. MERRITT, DIRECTOR ↓2X

iww
Enclosure

Copy notation   c: Legal Department

D. PERSONAL-BUSINESS LETTER
(in modified-block style and with international address and standard punctuation)

↓6X
→tab to centerpoint   July 15, 20-- ↓4X

Mr. Luis Fernandez, President
Arvon Industries, Inc.
21 St. Claire Avenue East
Toronto, Ontario M4T IL9
CANADA ↓2X

Dear Mr. Fernandez: ↓2X

As a former employee and present stockholder of Arvon Industries, I wish to protest the planned sale of the Consumer Products Division.

According to published reports, consumer products accounted for 19 percent of last year's corporate profits, and they are expected to account for even more this year. In addition, Dun & Bradstreet predicts that consumer products nationwide will outpace the general economy for the next five years.

I am concerned about the effect that this planned sale will have on overall corporate profits, on cash dividends for investors, and on the economy of Melbourne, where the two consumer-products plants are located.

Please ask your board of directors to reconsider this matter. ↓2X

→tab to centerpoint   Sincerely, ↓4X

Roger J. Michaelson

Return address   Roger J. Michaelson
901 East Benson, Apt. 3
Ft. Lauderdale, FL 33301

A. BUSINESS LETTER ON EXECUTIVE STATIONERY

(7¼" × 10½"; 1-inch side margins; with delivery notation)

Two Penn Plaza
10th Floor
New York, NY 10021-2298
Tel 212 904 2900
Fax 212 904 6630

Sweet's Group
McGraw-Hill Construction Information Group
A Division of The McGraw-Hill Companies

↓6X

July 18, 20--
↓4X

Mr. Rodney Eastwood
BBL Resources
52A Northern Ridge
Fayetteville, PA 17222
↓2X

Dear Rodney: ↓2X

I see no reason that we should continue to consider the locality
around Geraldton for our new plant. Even though the desirability of this site from an economic view is undeniable, there is
insufficient housing readily available for our workers.

In trying to control urban growth, the city has been turning
down the building permits for new housing or placing so many
restrictions on foreign investment as to make it too expensive.

Please continue to seek out other areas of exploration where we
might form a joint partnership.
↓2X

Sincerely, ↓4X

Arlyn J. Bunch

Arlyn J. Bunch
Vice President for O...
↓2X

mme
Delivery By Fax
notation

B. BUSINESS LETTER ON HALF-PAGE STATIONERY

(5½" × 8½"; 0.75-inch side margins)

1221 Avenue of the Americas
New York, NY 10020-1095

↓4X

July 18, 20--
↓4X

Business Week
A Division of The McGraw-Hill Companies

Mr. Rodney Eastwood
BBL Resources
52A Northern Ridge
Fayetteville, PA 17222
↓2X

Dear Rodney: ↓2X

We should continue considering Geraldton for our
new plant. Even though the desirability of this site
from an economic view is undeniable, there is
insufficient housing readily available.

Please continue to seek out other areas of exploration where we might form a joint partnership. ↓2X

Sincerely, ↓4X

Arlyn J. Bunch

Arlyn J. Bunch
Vice President for Operations ↓2X

adk

C. BUSINESS LETTER FORMATTED FOR A WINDOW ENVELOPE

APH

AMERICAN PRINTING HOUSE
FOR THE BLIND, INC.

↓6X

July 18, 20-- ↓3X

Mr. Rodney Eastwood
BBL Resources
52A Northern Ridge
Fayetteville, PA 17222
↓3X

Dear Rodney: ↓2X

I see no reason that we should continue to consider the locality around
Geraldton for our new plant. Even though the desirability of this site from an
economic view is undeniable, there is insufficient housing readily available
for our workers.

In trying to control urban growth, the city has been turning down the building
permits for new housing or placing so many restrictions on foreign investment
as to make it too expensive.

Please continue to seek out other areas of exploration where we might form a
joint partnership. ↓2X

Sincerely, ↓4X

Arlyn J. Bunch

Arlyn J. Bunch
Vice President for Operations ↓2X

woc

1839 Frankton Avenue   P.O. Box 6984   Louisville, Kentucky 90206-0389   502-895-2905   Fax 502-895-2350

D. MEMO

(with table and attachment notation)

↓6X   →tab

MEMO TO: Nancy Price, Executive Vice President ↓2X

FROM: Arlyn J. Bunch, Operations ↓2X

DATE: July 18, 20-- ↓2X

SUBJECT: New Plant Site ↓2X

As you can see from the attached letter, I've informed BBL Resources that I
see no reason why we should continue to consider the locality around
Geraldton for our new plant. Even though the desirability of this site from
an economic standpoint is undeniable, there is insufficient housing available.
In fact, as of June 25, the number of appropriate single-family houses listed
for sale within a 25-mile radius of Geraldton was as follows: ↓2X

Agent	Units
Belle Real Estate	123
Castleton Homes	11
Red Carpet	9
Geraldton Homes	5

↓1X

In addition, in trying to control urban growth, Geraldton has been either
turning down building permits for new housing or placing excessive restrictions on them.

Because of this deficiency of housing for our employees, we have no choice
but to look elsewhere. ↓2X

llw
Attachment Attachment
notation

Reference Manual

A. MULTIPAGE BUSINESS LETTER

(page 1; with on-arrival notation, international address, subject line, and table)

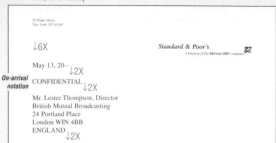

55 Water Street
New York, NY 10041

↓6X

Standard & Poor's
A Division of The McGraw-Hill Companies

May 13, 20-- ↓2X

On-arrival notation → CONFIDENTIAL ↓2X

Mr. Lester Thompson, Director
British Mutual Broadcasting
24 Portland Place
London WIN 4BB
ENGLAND ↓2X

Dear Mr. Thompson:

Subject line → Subject: International Study Tour ↓2X

I have been invited by the Federal Communications Commission to participate in a study of television news programming in European countries. The enclosed report explains the purpose of the study in detail.

I have been assigned to lead a study group through six European countries to gather firsthand information on this topic. In addition to me, our group will consist of the following members: ↓2X

INTERNATIONAL STUDY TOUR GROUP		
Name	Organization	Location
Mrs. Katherine Grant	WPQR-TV	Los Angeles, CA
Dr. Manuél Cruz	Miami Herald	Miami, FL
Mr. Richard Logan	Cable News Network	Atlanta, GA
Ms. Barbara Brooks	Associated Press	Chicago, IL

↓1X

Our initial plans are to spend at least one full day in each of the countries, meeting with the news programming staff of one or two of the major networks,

B. MULTIPAGE BUSINESS LETTER

(page 2; with company name; multiline list; enclosure, delivery, copy, postscript, and blind copy notations)

2

touring their facilities, viewing recent broadcasts, and getting a firsthand view of actual news operations. Our tentative itinerary calls for us to arrive at Heathrow Airport at 7:10 p.m. on Tuesday, July 27. Would it be possible for us to do the following:

1. Meet with various members of your staff sometime on July 28. We would be available from 8:30 a.m. until 1:30 p.m.

2. Receive a copy of your programming log for the week of July 26-30 and especially a minute-by-minute listing of the programming segments for your national news reporting.

I would appreciate your contacting Barbara Azar, our liaison, at 202.555.3943 to let us know whether we may study your operations on July 25. ↓2X

Sincerely, ↓2X

Company name → METRO BROADCASTING COMPANY ↓4X

Denise J. Watterson

Denise J. Watterson
General Manager ↓2X

Reference initials → rcp
Enclosure notation → Enclosures: FCC Report, Biographical Sketches
Delivery notation → By FedEx
Copy notation → c: Barbara Azar, Manuél Cruz ↓2X

Postscript notation → PS: The Federal Communications Commission will reimburse your organization for any expenses associated with our visit. ↓2X

Blind copy notation → bc: Public Relations Office, FTC

C. EMAIL MESSAGE IN MICROSOFT OUTLOOK/ INTERNET EXPLORER

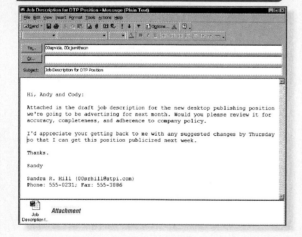

D. EMAIL MESSAGE IN NETSCAPE NAVIGATOR

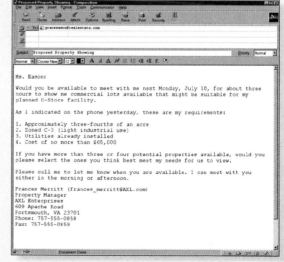

A. FORMATTING ENVELOPES

A standard large (No. 10) envelope is 9½ by 4⅛ inches. A standard small (No. 6¾) envelope is 6½ by 3⅝ inches. Although either address format shown below is acceptable, the format shown for the large envelope (all capital letters and no punctuation) is recommended by the U.S. Postal Service for mail that will be sorted by an electronic scanning device.

Window envelopes are often used in a word processing environment because of the difficulty of aligning envelopes correctly in some printers. A window envelope requires no formatting, since the letter is formatted and folded so that the inside address is visible through the window.

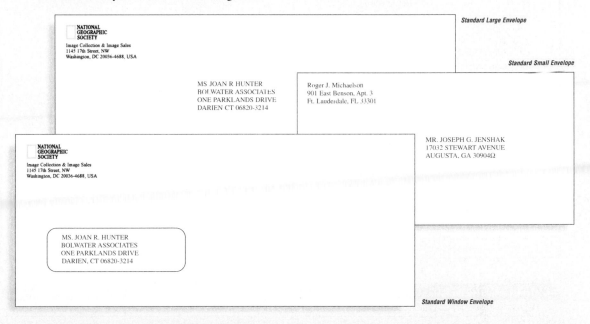

B. FOLDING LETTERS

To fold a letter for a large envelope:
1. Place the letter *face up* and fold up the bottom third.
2. Fold the top third down to 0.5 inch from the bottom edge.
3. Insert the last crease into the envelope first, with the flap facing up.

To fold a letter for a small envelope:
1. Place the letter *face up* and fold up the bottom half to 0.5 inch from the top.
2. Fold the right third over to the left.
3. Fold the left third over to 0.5 inch from the right edge.
4. Insert the last crease into the envelope first, with the flap facing up.

To fold a letter for a window envelope:
1. Place the letter *face down* with the letterhead at the top and fold the bottom third of the letter up.
2. Fold the top third down so that the address shows.
3. Insert the letter into the envelope so that the address shows through the window.

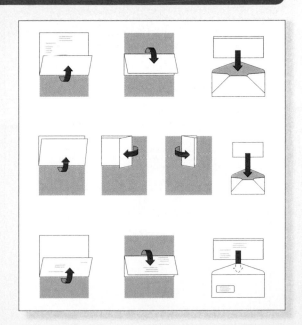

Reference Manual

A. OUTLINE

Set right tab at 0.3; left tabs at 0.4 and 0.7.

↓6X

14 pt **AN ANALYSIS OF THE SCOPE AND EFFECTIVENESS OF ONLINE ADVERTISING** ↓2X

12 pt↓ **The Status of Point-and-Click Selling** ↓2X

tab

Jonathan R. Evans ↓2X

January 19, 20-- ↓2X

I.   INTRODUCTION ↓2X

II. SCOPE AND TRENDS IN INTERNET ADVERTISING
    A. Internet Advertising
    B. Major Online Advertisers
    C. Positioning and Pricing
    D. Types of Advertising ↓2X

III. ADVERTISING EFFECTIVENESS
    A. The Banner Debate
    B. Increasing Advertising Effectiveness
    C. Measuring ROI ↓2X

IV. CONCLUSION

B. TITLE PAGE

center page↓

14 pt **AN ANALYSIS OF THE SCOPE AND EFFECTIVENESS OF ONLINE ADVERTISING** ↓2X

12 pt↓ **The Status of Point-and-Click Selling** ↓12X

Submitted to ↓2X

Luis Torres
General Manager
ViaWorld, International ↓12X

Prepared by ↓2X

Jonathan R. Evans
Assistant Marketing Manager
ViaWorld, International ↓2X

January 19, 20--

C. TRANSMITTAL MEMO

(with 2-line subject line and attachment notation)

↓6X

→ tab

MEMO TO: Luis Torres, General Manager ↓2X

FROM: Jonathan R. Evans, Assistant Marketing Manager *jre* ↓2X

DATE: January 19, 20-- ↓2X

SUBJECT: An Analysis of the Scope and Effectiveness of Online Advertising ↓2X

Here is the report analyzing the scope and effectiveness of Internet Advertising that you requested on January 5, 20--.

The report predicts that the total value of business-to-business e-commerce market will reach $1.3 trillion by 2003, up from $190 billion in 1999. New technologies aimed at increasing Internet ad interactivity and the adoption of standards for advertising response measurement and tracking will contribute to this increase. Unfortunately, as discussed in this report, the use of "rich media" and interactivity in Web advertising will create its own set of problems.

I enjoyed working on this assignment, Luis, and learned quite a bit from my analysis of the situation. Please let me know if you have any questions about the report. ↓2X

urs
Attachment

D. TABLE OF CONTENTS

Set left tab at 0.5; right dot-leader tab at 6.

↓6X

14 pt **CONTENTS** ↓2X

A. REPORT IN BUSINESS STYLE

(page 1; with footnotes and single-line list)

↓6X

Title 14 pt **AN ANALYSIS OF THE SCOPE AND EFFECTIVENESS OF ONLINE ADVERTISING** ↓2X

Subtitle 12 pt↓ **The Status of Point-and-Click Selling** ↓2X

Byline Jonathan R. Evans ↓2X

Date January 19, 20-- ↓2X

Side hd **INTRODUCTION** ↓2X

Over the past three years, the number of American households online has tripled, from an estimated 15 million in 1996 to 45 million in 1999. Jupiter Communications, predicts that by the year 2003, 70 million households, representing about 62% of all U.S. households, will be online. Online business has grown in tandem with the expanding number of Internet users. Forrester Research Inc. predicts that the total value of business-to-business e-commerce will reach $109 billion in 1999 and is likely to reach $1.3 trillion by 2003.[1] ↓2X

Para hd **Uncertainty**. The uncertainties surrounding advertising on the Internet remain one of the major impediments to the expansion. Dating from just 1994 when the first banner ads appeared on the Hotwired home page, the young Internet advertising industry is today in a state of flux. ↓2X

Some analysts argue that advertising on the Internet can and should follow the same principles as advertising on television and other visual media. Others contend that advertising on the Internet should reflect the unique characteristics of this new medium. ↓2X

Reasons for Not Advertising Online. A recent Association of National Advertisers survey found two main reasons cited for not advertising online.[2] ↓2X

1. The difficulty of determining return on investment
2. The lack of reliable tracking and measurement data

Footnotes
[1] George Anders, "Buying Frenzy," *Wall Street Journal*, July 12, 1999, p. R6.
[2] "eStats: Advertising Revenues and Trends," *eMarketer Home Page*, August 11, 1999, http:www.emarketer.com/estats/ad (January 7, 2000).

B. REPORT IN BUSINESS STYLE

(page 3; with long quotation and table)

3

who argue that banners have a strong potential for advertising effectiveness point out that it is not the banner format itself which presents a problem to advertising effectiveness, but rather the quality of the banner and the attention to its placement. According to Mike Windsor, president of Ogilvy Interactive: ↓2X

indent 0.5"→ *Long quotation* It's more a case of bad banner ads, just like there are bad television ads. The space itself has huge potential. As important as using the space within the banner creatively is to aim it effectively. Unlike broadcast media, the Web offers advertisers the opportunity to reach a specific audience based on data gathered about who is surfing at a particular site and what their interests are.[1] *←indent 0.5"*

Thus, while some analysts continue to argue that the banner advertisement is passé, there is little evidence of its abandonment. Instead ad agencies are focusing on increasing the banner's effectiveness. ↓2X

SCOPE AND TRENDS IN ONLINE ADVERTISING ↓2X

Starting from zero in 1994, analysts agree that the volume of Internet advertising spending has risen rapidly. However, as indicated in Table 3, analysts provide a wide range of the exact amount of such advertising. ↓2X

TABLE 3. INTERNET ADVERTISING 1998 Estimates ↓1X	
Source	**Estimate**
Internet Advertising Board	$1.92 billion
Forester	1.30 billion
IDC	1.20 billion
Burst! Media	560 million

Source: "A Look at 'Upfront' Trends with eMarketer for Research Report," *Advertising Age*, May 3, 1999, p. 24. ↓1X

The differences in estimates of total Web advertising spending is generally attributed to the different methodologies used by the research agencies to

[1] Lisa Napoli, "Banner Ads Are Under the Gun—And On the Move," *New York Times*, June 17, 1999, p. D1.

C. REPORT IN ACADEMIC STYLE

(page 1; with endnotes and multiline list)

↓3DS

14 pt **AN ANALYSIS OF THE SCOPE AND EFFECTIVENESS OF ONLINE ADVERTISING** ↓1DS

12 pt↓ **The Status of Point-and-Click Selling** ↓1DS

Jonathan R. Evans ↓1DS

January 19, 20-- ↓1DS

INTRODUCTION

Over the past three years, the number of American households online has tripled, from an estimated 15 million in 1996 to 45 million in 1999. Jupiter Communications, predicts that by the year 2003, 70 million households, representing about 62% of all U.S. households, will be online. Online business has grown in tandem with the expanding number of Internet users. Forrester Research Inc. predicts that the total value of business-to-business e-commerce will reach $109 billion in 1999 and is likely to reach $1.3 trillion by 2003.[i]

Reasons for Not Advertising Online. A recent Association of National Advertisers survey found two main reasons cited for not advertising online:[ii]

1. The difficulty of determining return on investment, especially in terms of repeat business.
2. The lack of reliable tracking and measurement data

Some analysts argue that advertising on the Internet can and should follow the same principles as advertising on television.[iii] Other visual media

D. REPORT IN ACADEMIC STYLE

(last page; with long quotation and endnotes)

14

advertising effectiveness, but rather the quality of the banner and the attention to its placement. According to Mike Windsor, president of Ogilvy Interactive:

indent 0.5" *Long quotation* It's more a case of bad banner ads, just like there are bad television ads. The space itself has huge potential. As important as using the space within the banner creatively is to aim it effectively. Unlike broadcast media, the Web offers advertisers the opportunity to reach a specific audience based on data gathered about who is surfing at a particular site and what their interests are.[vii] *←indent 0.5"*

From the advertiser's perspective, the most effective Internet ads do more than just deliver information to the consumer and grab the consumer's attention—they also gather information about consumers (e.g., through "cookies" and other methodologies). From the consumer's perspective, this type of interactivity may represent an intrusion and an invasion of privacy. There appears to be a shift away from the ad-supported model and toward the transaction model, wherein users pay for the content they want and the specific transactions they perform.

Endnotes
[i] George Anders, "Buying Frenzy," *Wall Street Journal*, July 12, 1999, p. R6.
[ii] "eStats: Advertising Revenues and Trends," *eMarketer Home Page*, August 11, 1999, http:www.emarketer.com/estats/ad (January 7, 2000).
[iii] Bradley Johnson, "Nielsen/NetRatings Index Shows 4% Rise in Web Ads," *Advertising Age*, July 19, 1999, p. 18.
[iv] Tom Hyland, "Web Advertising: A Year of Growth," *Internet Advertising Board Home Page*, November 13, 1999, http:www.iab.net/advertise (January 8, 2000).
[v] Adrian Mand, "Click Here: Free Ride Doles Out Freebies to Ad Surfers," *Brandweek*, March 8, 1999, p. 30.
[vi] Andrea Petersen, "High Price of Internet Banner Ads Slips Amid Increase in Web Sites," *Wall Street Journal*, March 2, 1999, p. B20.
[vii] Lisa Napoli, "Banner Ads Are Under the Gun—And On the Move," *New York Times*, June 17, 1999, p. D1.

Reference Manual

A. LEFT-BOUND REPORT IN BUSINESS STYLE

(page 1; with endnotes and single-line list)

---

left margin: 1.75"   right margin: *default* (1.25")

↓6X

14 pt

AN ANALYSIS OF THE SCOPE AND
EFFECTIVENESS OF ONLINE ADVERTISING ↓2X

12 pt↓

The Status of Point-and-Click Selling ↓2X

Jonathan R. Evans ↓2X

January 19, 20-- ↓2X
↓2X

INTRODUCTION ↓2X

Over the past three years, the number of American households online has tripled, from an estimated 15 million in 1996 to 45 million in 1999. Jupiter Communications, predicts that by the year 2003, 70 million households, representing about 62% of all U.S. households, will be online. Online business has grown in tandem with the expanding number of Internet users. Forrester Research Inc. predicts that the total value of business-to-business e-commerce will reach $109 billion in 1999 and is likely to reach $1.3 trillion by 2003.[i] ↓2X

Uncertainty. The uncertainties surrounding advertising on the Internet remain one of the major impediments to the expansion. Dating from just 1994 when the first banner ads appeared on the Hotwired home page, the young Internet advertising industry is today in a state of flux. ↓2X

Some analysts argue that advertising on the Internet can and should follow the same principles as advertising on television and other visual media. Others contend that advertising on the Internet should reflect the unique characteristics of this new medium. ↓2X

Reasons for Not Advertising Online. A recent Association of National Advertisers survey found two main reasons cited for not advertising online:[ii] ↓2X

1. The difficulty of determining return on investment
2. The lack of reliable tracking and measurement data

B. BIBLIOGRAPHY

(For business or academic style using either endnotes or footnotes)

↓6X

hanging indent

12 pt↓   14 pt **BIBLIOGRAPHY** ↓2X

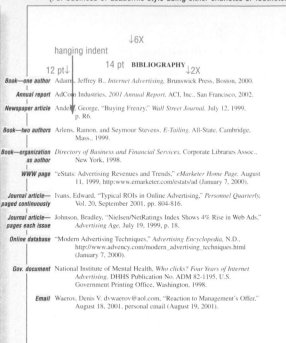

Book—one author Adams, Jeffrey B., *Internet Advertising*, Brunswick Press, Boston, 2000.

Annual report AdCom Industries, *2001 Annual Report*, ACI, Inc., San Francisco, 2002.

Newspaper article Anderff, George, "Buying Frenzy," *Wall Street Journal*, July 12, 1999, p. R6.

Book—two authors Arlens, Ramon, and Seymour Stevens, *E-Tailing*, All-State, Cambridge, Mass., 1999.

Book—organization as author *Directory of Business and Financial Services*, Corporate Libraries Assoc., New York, 1998.

WWW page "eStats: Advertising Revenues and Trends," *eMarketer Home Page*, August 11, 1999, http:www.emarketer.com/estats/ad (January 7, 2000).

Journal article— paged continuously Ivans, Edward, "Typical ROIs in Online Advertising," *Personnel Quarterly*, Vol. 20, September 2001, pp. 804-816.

Journal article— pages each issue Johnson, Bradley, "Nielsen/NetRatings Index Shows 4% Rise in Web Ads," *Advertising Age*, July 19, 1999, p. 18.

Online database "Modern Advertising Techniques," *Advertising Encyclopedia*, N.D., http://www.advency.com/modern_advertising_techniques.html (January 7, 2000).

Gov. document National Institute of Mental Health, *Who clicks? Four Years of Internet Advertising*, DHHS Publication No. ADM 82-1195, U.S. Government Printing Office, Washington, 1998.

Email Waerov, Denis V. dvwaerov@aol.com, "Reaction to Management's Offer," August 18, 2001, personal email (August 19, 2001).

C. MEMO REPORT

(page 1, with single-line list)

↓6X
→tab
MEMO TO: Luis Torres, General Manager ↓2X

FROM: Jonathan R. Evans, Assistant Marketing Manager *jre* ↓2X

DATE: January 19, 20-- ↓2X

SUBJECT: An Analysis of the Scope and Effectiveness of Online Advertising ↓2X

According to a July 12, 1999, *Wall Street* Journal article, over the past three years, the number of American households online has tripled, from an estimated 15 million in 1996 to 45 million in 1999. Jupiter Communications, predicts that by the year 2003, 70 million households, representing about 62% of all U.S. households, will be online. Online business has grown in tandem with the expanding number of Internet users. Forrester Research Inc. predicts that the total value of business-to-business e-commerce will reach $109 billion in 1999 and is likely to reach $1.3 trillion by 2003.

UNCERTAINTY

The uncertainties surrounding advertising on the Internet remain one of the major impediments to the expansion. Dating from just 1994 when the first banner ads appeared on the Hotwired home page, the young Internet advertising industry is today in a state of flux.

Some analysts argue that advertising on the Internet can and should follow the same principles as advertising on television and other visual media. Others contend that advertising on the Internet should reflect the unique characteristics of this new medium.

A recent Association of National Advertisers survey found two main reasons cited for not advertising online:

1. The difficulty of determining return on investment
2. The lack of reliable tracking and measurement data

D. REPORTS: SPECIAL FEATURES

MARGINS AND SPACING. Use a 2" top margin for the first page of each section of a report (for example, the table of contents, first page of the body, and bibliography page) and a 1" top margin for other pages. Use default side margins (1.25") and bottom margins (1") for all pages. If the report is going to be bound on the left, add 0.5" to the left margin. Single-space business reports and double-space academic reports.

HEADINGS. Center the report title in 14-point font (press **ENTER** to space down before switching to 12-point font). Single-space multiline report titles in a single-spaced report and double-space multiline titles in a double-spaced report. Leave 1 blank line before and after all parts of a heading block (consisting of the title, subtitle, author, and/or date) and format all lines in bold.

Leave 1 blank line before and after side headings and format in bold, beginning at the left margin. Format paragraph headings in bold; begin at the left margin for single-spaced reports and indent for double-spaced reports. The text follows on the same line, preceded by a period and 1 space.

CITATIONS. For business and academic reports, format citations using your word processor's footnote (or endnote) feature. For reports formatted in APA or MLA style, use the format shown on page R-10.

Reference Manual

A. REPORT IN APA STYLE
(page 3; with author/year citations)

top, bottom, and side margins: 1″
Double-space throughout.

header — Online Advertising 3

An Analysis of the Scope and Effectiveness

of Online Advertising

Jonathan R. Evans

main hd. — Introduction

Over the past three years, the number of American households online has tripled, from an estimated 15 million in 1996 to 45 million in 1999. Jupiter Communications, predicts that by the year 2003, 70 million households, representing about 62% of all U.S. households, will be online (Napoli, 1999). Online business has grown in tandem with the expanding number of Internet users. Forrester Research Inc. predicts that the total value of business-to-business e-commerce will reach $109 billion in 1999 and is likely to reach $1.3 trillion by 2003 (Arlens & Stevens, 1999). ↓1DS

subhd. — Uncertainty

The uncertainties surrounding advertising on the Internet remain one of the major impediments to the expansion. Dating from just 1994 when the first banner ads appeared on the Hotwired home page, the young Internet advertising industry is today in a state of flux.

Some analysts argue that advertising on the Internet can and should follow the same principles as advertising on television and other visual media ("eStats," 1999). Others contend that advertising on the Internet should reflect

B. REFERENCES IN APA STYLE

top, bottom, and side margins: 1″
Double-space throughout.

header — Online Advertising 14

References

Adams, J. B. (2000). *Internet advertising*. Boston: Brunswick Press.

AdCom Industries. (2002). *2001 annual report*. San Francisco: ACI, Inc.

Anders, G. (1999, July 12). Buying frenzy. *Wall Street Journal*, p. R6.

Arlens, R., & Stevens, S. (1999). *E-tailing*. Cambridge, MA: All-State.

Directory of business and financial services. (1998). New York: Corporate Libraries Association.

eStats: Advertising revenues and trends. (n.d.). New York: eMarketer. Retrieved August 11, 1999 from the World Wide Web: http:www.emarketer.com/estats/ad.

Ivans, E. (2001). Typical ROIs in online advertising. *Personnel Quarterly, 20*, 804-816.

Johnson, B. (1999, July 19). Nielsen/NetRatings Index shows 4% rise in Web ads. *Advertising Age, 39*, 18.

Napoli, L. (1999, June 17). Banner ads are under the gun—And on the move. *New York Times*, p. D1.

National Institute of Mental Health. (1998). *Who clicks? Four years of Internet advertising* (DHHS Publication No. ADM 82-1195). Washington,

C. REPORT IN MLA STYLE
(page 1; with author/page citations)

top, bottom, and side margins: 1″
Double-space throughout.

header — Evans 1

Jonathan R. Evans

Professor Inman

Management 302

19 January 20--

An Analysis of the Scope and Effectiveness

of Online Advertising

Over the past three years, the number of American households online has tripled, from an estimated 15 million in 1996 to 45 million in 1999. Jupiter Communications, predicts that by the year 2003, 70 million households, representing about 62% of all U.S. households, will be online (Napoli D1). Online business has grown in tandem with the expanding number of Internet users. Forrester Research Inc. predicts that the total value of business-to-business e-commerce will reach $109 billion in 1999 and is likely to reach $1.3 trillion by 2003 (Arlens & Stevens 376-379).

The uncertainties surrounding advertising on the Internet remain one of the major impediments to the expansion. Dating from just 1994 when the first banner ads appeared on the Hotwired home page, the young Internet advertising industry is today in a state of flux.

Some analysts argue that advertising on the Internet can and should follow the same principles as advertising on television and other visual media ("eStats"). Others contend that advertising on the Internet should reflect the

D. WORKS CITED IN MLA STYLE

top, bottom, and side margins: 1″
Double-space throughout.

header — Evans 13

Works Cited

Adams, Jeffrey B. *Internet Advertising*. Boston: Brunswick Press, 2000.

AdCom Industries. *2001 Annual Report*. San Francisco: ACI, Inc., 2002.

Anders, George. "Buying Frenzy," *Wall Street Journal*, July 12, 1999, p. R6.

Arlens, Ramon, and Seymour Stevens. *E-Tailing*. Cambridge, MA: All-State, 1999.

hanging indent

Corporate Libraries Association. *Directory of Business and Financial Services*. New York: Corporate Libraries Association, 1998.

"eStats: Advertising Revenues and Trends." *eMarketer Home Page*. 11 Aug. 1999. 7 Jan. 2000. http:www.emarketer.com/estats/ad.

Ivans, Edward. "Typical ROIs in Online Advertising." *Personnel Quarterly* Sep. 2001: 804-816.

Johnson, Bradley. "Nielsen/NetRatings Index Shows 4% Rise in Web Ads." *Advertising Age* 19 Jul. 1999: 18.

Napoli, Lisa. "Banner Ads Are Under the Gun—And On the Move." *New York Times* 17 Jun. 1999: D1.

National Institute of Mental Health. *Who Clicks? Four Years of Internet Advertising*. DHHS Publication No. ADM 82-1195. Washington, DC: GPO, 1998.

Reference Manual

A. MEETING AGENDA

First type list unformatted; then apply numbering feature.

↓6X

14 pt **MILES HARDWARE EXECUTIVE COMMITTEE** ↓2X

12 pt↓ **Meeting Agenda** ↓2X

June 7, 20--, 3 p.m. ↓2X

1. Call to order ↓2X

2. Approval of minutes of May 5 meeting

3. Progress report on building addition and parking lot restrictions (Norman Hodges and Anthony Pascarelli)

4. May 15 draft of five-Year Plan

5. Review of National Hardware Association annual convention

6. Employee grievance filed by Ellen Burrows (John Landstrom)

7. New expense-report forms (Anne Richards)

8. Announcements

9. Adjournment

B. MINUTES OF A MEETING

Format body as a two-column open table; manually adjust column widths as needed.

↓6X

14 pt **RESOURCE COMMITTEE** ↓2X

12 pt↓ **Minutes of the Meeting** ↓2X

March 13, 20-- ↓2X

ATTENDANCE	The Resource Committee met on March 13, 20--, at the Airport Sheraton in Portland, Oregon, with all members were present. Michael Davis, chairperson, called the meeting to order at 2:30 p.m. ↓2X
APPROVAL OF MINUTES	The minutes of the January 27 meeting were read and approved.
OLD BUSINESS	The members of the committee reviewed the sales brochure on electronic copyboards and agreed to purchase one for the conference room. Cynthia Giovanni will secure quotations from at least two suppliers.
NEW BUSINESS	The committee reviewed a request from the Purchasing Department for three new computers. After extensive discussion regarding the appropriate use of the computers and softwre to be purchased, the committee approved the request.
ADJOURNMENT	The meeting was adjourned at 4:45 p.m. ↓2X

Respectfully submitted, ↓4X

D. S. Madsen

D. S. Madsen, Secretary

C. ITINERARY

Format body as a two-column open table; manually adjust column widths as needed.

↓6X

14 pt **ITINERARY** ↓2X

12 pt↓ **For Arlene Gilsdorf** ↓2X

March 12-15, 20-- ↓2X

THURSDAY, MARCH 12 ↓2X

5:10 p.m.-7:06 p.m.	Flight from Detroit to Portland; Northwest 83 (Phone: 800-555-1212); e-ticket; Seat 8D; nonstop; dinner ↓2X
	Jack Weatherford (Home: 503-555-8029; Office: 503-555-7631) will meet your flight on Thursday, provide transportation during your visit, and return you to the airport on Saturday morning. ↓2X
	Airport Sheraton (503-555-4032) King-sized bed, nonsmoking room; late arrival guaranteed (Reservation No. 30ZM6-02) ↓2X

FRIDAY, MARCH 13

9 a.m.-5:30 p.m.	Portland Sales Meeting 1931 Executive Way, Suite 10 Portland (503-555-7631)
Evening	On your own

SATURDAY, MARCH 14

7:30 a.m.-2:47 p.m.	Flight from Portland to Detroit; Northwest 360; e-ticket; Seat 9a; nonstop; breakfast

D. LEGAL DOCUMENT

Set left tabs at 1" and 3".

↓3DS

14 pt **POWER OF ATTORNEY** ↓1DS

12 pt↓ KNOW ALL MEN BY THESE PRESENTS that I, ATTORNEY LEE FERNANDEZ, of the City of Tulia, County of Swisher, State of Texas, do hereby appoint my son, Robert Fernandez, of this City, County, and State as my attorney-in-fact to act in my name, place, and stead as my agent in the management of my business operating transactions.

I give and grant unto my said attorney full power and authority to do and perform every act and thing requisite and necessary to be done in the said management as fully, to all intents and purposes, as I might or could do if personally present, with full power of revocation, hereby ratifying all that my said attorney shall lawfully do.

IN WITNESS WHEREOF, I have hereunto set my hand and seal this thirteenth day of April, 20--. ↓2DS

→tab to centerpoint _____ (L.S.) ↓1DS

SIGNED and affirmed in the presence of: ↓2DS

_____ ↓2DS

_____

footer Page 1 of 1

A. RESUME

Format body as a two-column open table; manually adjust column widths as needed.

↓6X

14 pt   **TERRY M. MARTINA** ↓2X

12 pt ↓   **250 Maxwell Avenue, Boulder, CO 80305**
Phone: 303-555-9311; email: tmartina@ecc.edu ↓1X

↓1X

OBJECTIVE	Position in resort management anywhere in Colorado ↓2X
EDUCATION	A. A. in hotel management to be awarded May 2001 Edgewood Community College, Boulder, CO
EXPERIENCE	*Assistant Manager, Burger King Restaurant* Boulder, CO: 1999-Present • Achieved grade point average of 3.1 (on 4.0 scale). • Received Board of Regent tuition scholarship. • Financed all college expenses through savings, scholarships, and part-time work. *Student Intern, Ski Valley Haven* Aspen, CO: September-December 2000 • Worked as an assistant to the night manager of 200-room ski resort. • Gained practical experience in operating First-Guest management system. • Was in charge of producing daily occupancy reports.
PERSONAL	• Speak and write fluent Spanish • Competent in Microsoft Office 2000 • Secretary of ECC Hospitality Services Association • Special Olympics volunteer: Summer 2000
REFERENCES	Available upon request

B. APPLICATION LETTER

↓6X

March 1, 20-- ↓4X

Mr. Lou Mansfield, Director
Human Resources Department
Rocky Resorts International
P.O. Box 1412
Denver, CO 80214 ↓2X

Dear Mr. Mansfield: ↓2X

Please consider me an applicant for the position of concierge for Suite Retreat, as advertised in last Sunday's *Denver Times*.

I will receive my A.A. degree in hotel administration from Edgewood Community College in May and will be available for full-time employment immediately. In addition to my extensive coursework in hospitality services and business, I've had experience in working for a ski lodge similar to Suite Retreats in Aspen. As a lifelong resident of Colorado and an avid skier, I would be able to provide your guests with any information they request.

After you've reviewed my enclosed resume, I would appreciate having an opportunity to discuss with you why I believe I have the right qualifications and personality to serve as your concierge. I can be reached at 303-555-9311. ↓2X

Sincerely, ↓4X

Terry M. Martina

Terry M. Martina
250 Maxwell Avenue, Apt. 8
Boulder, CO 80305 ↓2X

Enclosure

C. PLACING INFORMATION ON PRINTED LINES

Because of the difficulty of aligning copy on a printed line with a computer and printer, lined forms such as job-application forms are most efficiently completed on a typewriter.

When typing on a lined form, use the typewriter's variable line spacer to adjust the paper so that the line is in the position that a row of underlines would occupy. (On many machines, this is accomplished by pressing in the left platen knob.)

Do not leave any lines for requested information blank; use *N/A* ("not applicable") if necessary. Because of space limitations, it may be necessary to abbreviate some words.

Because first impressions are important, ensure that all your employment documents are in correct format, are neat in appearance, and are free from errors.

D. JOB-APPLICATION FORM

(first page)

ROCKY RESORTS INTERNATIONAL
P.O. Box 1412   Denver, CO 80218
Employment Application

POSITION APPLIED FOR _Concierge_   DATE OF APPLICATION _3/18/00_

TYPE OF EMPLOYMENT DESIRED ☒ Full-time ☐ Part-time ☐ Temporary ☐ Co-op/Internship

NAME _Martina_   _Terry_   _M_
       LAST   FIRST   MI

ADDRESS _250 Maxwell Avenue, Apt. B_ _Boulder_ _CO_ _80305_
        STREET   CITY   STATE   ZIP

TELEPHONE _303-555-9311_   SOCIAL SECURITY NO. _247-72-8431_

If you are under 18, can you furnish a work permit? .... _N/A_ .... ☐ Yes ... ☐ No

Have you ever worked here before? .... ☒ Yes ... ☐ No

Are you legally eligible for employment in this country? .... ☒ Yes ... ☐ No

Have you been convicted of a felony within the past seven years? .... ☐ Yes ... ☒ No

If yes, please explain _____ _N/A_ _____

EDUCATION (most recent first)

Institution	City/State	Degree/Major	Dates
Edgewood Community College, Boulder, CO		A.A.—Hotel Admin.	2000-02
Durango High School, Durango, CO		Diploma	1997-2000

WORK EXPERIENCE (most recent first)

Organization	City/State	Position	Dates (inclusive)
Burger King Restaurant	Boulder, CO	Asst. Mgr.	1999-present
Ski Valley Haven	Aspen, CO	Intern	Sep-Dec 1999

AN EQUAL OPPORTUNITY EMPLOYER

Reference Manual

A. BOXED TABLE *(Default Style)*

(with subtitle, braced headings, total line, and table note.)

center page ↓

Title	12 pt ↓ **AUSTIN-REEVES PRINTER DEPOT**				
Subtitle	**Sales Through September 2001**				
	(000s omitted) ↓1X				

Product	Year-to-Date Sales		Prior-Year Sales	
↓1X	2002	2001	2000	1999
Dot matrix	$ 5	$ 14	$ 19	$ 28
Ink-jet: color	188	423	569	841
Ink-jet: color portable	4	7	6	24
Ink-jet: black and white	146	200	273	588
Printer and copier combination	1,000	1,184	1,622	2,054
Black-and-white laser: standard	144	316	389	507
Black-and-white laser: premium	2,591	1,636	2368	87
Color laser	6	0	0	0
Totals	$4,084	$3,780	$5,246	$4,129
Note: Year-to-date sales have increased 7.4%.				

Labels: Column hds (↓1X), Braced column hd, Body, Total line, Table note

B. OPEN TABLE

(with subtitle, blocked column headings, and 2-line heading)

First, format the table in default (boxed) style. Then delete all borders.

center page ↓

12 pt ↓ **SUITE RETREAT**
New Lodging Rates ↓1X

Location	Rack Rate	Discount Rate	Saving
Bozeman, Montana	$ 95.75	$ 91.50	4.4%
Chicago, Illinois	159.00	139.50	12.3%
Dallas, Texas	249.50	219.00	12.2%
Las Vegas, Nevada	98.50	89.95	8.7%
Los Angeles, California	179.00	139.00	22.3%
Minneapolis, Minnesota	115.00	95.00	17.4%
New York City, New York	227.50	175.00	23.1%
Orlando, Florida	105.75	98.50	6.3%
Portland, Maine	93.50	93.50	0.0%
Seattle, Washington	143.75	125.75	12.5%

↓1X (below Location heading)

C. RULED TABLE

(with table number and centered column headings)

2

an effort to reduce errors and provide increased customer support, we have recently added numerous additional telephone support services, some of which are available 24 hours a day and others available during the work day. These are shown in Table 2. ↓2X

12 pt ↓ **Table 2. COMPUTER SUPPLIES SUPPORT SERVICES** ↓1X

Support Service	Telephone	Hours
Product literature	800-555-3867	6 a.m. to 5 p.m.
Replacement parts	303-555-3388	24 hours a day
Technical documentation	408-555-3309	24 hours a day
Troubleshooting	800-555-8277	10 a.m. to 5 p.m.
Printer drivers	800-555-2377	6 a.m. to 5 p.m.
Software notes	800-555-3496	24 hours a day
Technical support	800-555-1205	24 hours a day
Hardware information	303-555-4289	6 a.m. to 5 p.m.

↓1X

We hope you will take advantages of these additional services to ensure that the computer hardware and software you purchase from Computer Supplies continues to provide you the quality and service you have come to expect from our company.

Sincerely,

Douglas Pullis

Douglas Pullis
General Manager

cds

First, format the table in default (boxed) style. Then delete all borders. Finally, add borders to the top and bottom of the column-heading row and to the bottom of the last row of the body of the table.

D. TABLES: SPECIAL FEATURES

VERTICAL PLACEMENT. Vertically center a table that appears on a page by itself. Leave 1 blank line before and after a table appearing with other text.

TITLE BLOCK. Center and bold all lines of the title block, typing the title in all caps and the subtitle in upper- and lowercase. If a table has a number, type the word *Table* in initial caps. Follow the table number with a period and 1 space.

COLUMN HEADINGS. Center column headings if *all* columns consist of text (e.g., words, phone numbers, or years). Block column headings if columns consist of text (left-aligned) and quantities (right-aligned). Regardless of the type of column, center braced headings. If the column headings do not take the same number of lines, align the headings at the bottom (by choosing the *bottom alignment* option). Use bold upper- and lowercase.

COLUMN CAPITALIZATION. Capitalize only the first word and proper nouns in column entries.

PERCENTAGES AND DOLLARS. Repeat the % sign for each number in a column (unless the heading identifies the data as percentages). Insert the $ sign only before the first amount and before a total amount. Align the $ sign with the longest amount in the column, inserting spaces after the $ sign as needed (leaving 2 spaces for each digit and 1 space for each comma).

TOTAL LINE. Add a border above a total line. Use the word *Total* or *Totals* as appropriate.

A. FORMATTING BUSINESS FORMS

Many business forms can be created and filled in by using templates that are provided within commercial word processing software. Template forms can be used "as is" or they can be edited. Templates can also be used to create customized forms for any business.

When a template is opened, the form is displayed on screen. The user can then fill in the necessary information, including personalized company information. Data is entered into cells or fields and you can move quickly from field to field with a single keystroke—usually by pressing Tab or Enter.

B. U.S. POSTAL SERVICE ABBREVIATIONS

(for States, Territories, and Canadian Provinces)

States and Territories

Alabama	AL	North Carolina	NC
Alaska	AK	North Dakota	ND
Arizona	AZ	Ohio	OH
Arkansas	AR	Oklahoma	OK
California	CA	Oregon	OR
Colorado	CO	Pennsylvania	PA
Connecticut	CT	Puerto Rico	PR
Delaware	DE	Rhode Island	RI
District of Columbia	DC	South Carolina	SC
Florida	FL	South Dakota	SD
Georgia	GA	Tennessee	TN
Guam	GU	Texas	TX
Hawaii	HI	Utah	UT
Idaho	ID	Vermont	VT
Illinois	IL	Virgin Islands	VI
Indiana	IN	Virginia	VA
Iowa	IA	Washington	WA
Kansas	KS	West Virginia	WV
Kentucky	KY	Wisconsin	WI
Louisiana	LA	Wyoming	WY
Maine	ME		
Maryland	MD	**Canadian Provinces**	
Massachusetts	MA	Alberta	AB
Michigan	MI	British Columbia	BC
Minnesota	MN	Labrador	LB
Mississippi	MS	Manitoba	MB
Missouri	MO	New Brunswick	NB
Montana	MT	Newfoundland	NF
Nebraska	NE	Northwest Territories	NT
Nevada	NV	Nova Scotia	NS
New Hampshire	NH	Ontario	ON
New Jersey	NJ	Prince Edward Island	PE
New Mexico	NM	Quebec	PQ
New York	NY	Saskatchewan	SK
		Yukon Territory	YT

C. PROOFREADERS' MARKS

Proofreaders' Marks		Draft	Final Copy	Proofreaders' Marks		Draft	Final Copy
⌒	Omit space	data base	database	SS	Single-space	first line / second line	first line second line
∨ or ∧	Insert	if he's not going	if he's not going,	ds	Double-space	first line / second line	first line / second line
≡	Capitalize	Maple street	Maple Street		Move right	Please send	Please send
ℓ	Delete	a final draft	a draft		Move left	May I	May I
#	Insert space	allready to	all ready to	∿	Bold	Column Heading	**Column Heading**
when / ⸺	Change word	and if you	and when you	ital	Italic	Time magazine	*Time* magazine
/	Use lowercase letter	our President	our president	u/l	Underline	Time magazine	Time magazine readers
¶	Paragraph	Most of the	Most of the	♂	Move as shown	readers will see	will see
⋯	Don't delete	a true story	a true story				
○	Spell out	the only ①	the only one				
∽	Transpose	they all see	they see all				

Language Arts for Business

(50 "must-know" rules)

PUNCTUATION

COMMAS

RULE 1 ▶
, direct address
(L. 21)

Use commas before and after a name used in direct address.

Thank you, John, for responding to my email so quickly.

Ladies and gentlemen, the program has been canceled.

RULE 2 ▶
, independent clause
(L. 27)

Use a comma between independent clauses joined by a coordinate conjunction (unless both clauses are short).

Ellen left her job with IBM, and she and her sister went to Paris.

But: Ellen left her job with IBM and went to Paris with her sister.

But: John drove and I navigated.

Note: An independent clause is one that can stand alone as a complete sentence. The most common coordinate conjunctions are *and, but, or,* and *nor.*

RULE 3 ▶
, introductory expression
(L. 27)

Use a comma after an introductory expression (unless it is a short prepositional phrase).

Before we can make a decision, we must have all the facts.

But: In 2000 our nation elected a new president.

Note: An introductory expression is a group of words that come before the subject and verb of the independent clause. Common prepositions are *to, in, on, of, at, by, for,* and *with.*

RULE 4 ▶
, direct quotation
(L. 41)

Use a comma before and after a direct quotation.

James said, "I shall return," and then left.

RULE 5 ▶
, date
(L. 57)

Use a comma before *and after* the year in a complete date.

We will arrive on June 2, 2001, for the conference.

But: We will arrive on June 2 for the conference.

RULE 6 ▶
, place
(L. 57)

Use a comma before *and after* a state or country that follows a city (but not before a ZIP Code).

Joan moved to Vancouver, British Columbia, in May.

Send the package to Douglasville, GA 30135, by Express Mail.

But: Send the package to Georgia by Express Mail.

RULE 7 ▶ , series (L. 61)	**Use a comma between each item in a series of three or more.** We need to order paper, toner, and font cartridges for the printer. They saved their work, exited their program, and turned off their computers when they finished. **Note:** Do not use a comma after the last item in a series.
RULE 8 ▶ , transitional expression (L. 61)	**Use a comma before and after a transitional expression or independent comment.** It is critical, therefore, that we finish the project on time. Our present projections, you must admit, are inadequate. *But:* You must admit our present projections are inadequate. **Note:** Examples of transitional expressions and independent comments are *in addition to, therefore, however, on the other hand, as a matter of fact,* and *unfortunately.*
RULE 9 ▶ , nonessential expression (L. 71)	**Use a comma before and after a nonessential expression.** Andre, who was there, can verify the statement. *But:* Anyone who was there can verify the statement. Van's first book, *Crisis of Management,* was not discussed. Van's book *Crisis of Management* was not discussed. **Note:** A nonessential expression is a group of words that may be omitted without changing the basic meaning of the sentence. Always examine the noun or pronoun that comes before the expression to determine whether the noun needs the expression to complete its meaning. If it does, the expression is *essential* and does *not* take a comma.
RULE 10 ▶ , adjacent adjectives (L. 71)	**Use a comma between two adjacent adjectives that modify the same noun.** We need an intelligent, enthusiastic individual for this job. *But:* Please order a new bulletin board for our main conference room. **Note:** Do not use a comma after the second adjective. Also, do not use a comma if the first adjective modifies the combined idea of the second adjective and the noun (for example, *bulletin board* and *conference room* in the second example above).

SEMICOLONS

RULE 11 ▶ ; no conjunction (L. 97)	**Use a semicolon to separate two closely related independent clauses that are *not* joined by a conjunction (such as *and, but, or,* or *nor*).** Management favored the vote; stockholders did not. *But:* Management favored the vote, but stockholders did not.
RULE 12 ▶ ; series (L. 97)	**Use a semicolon to separate three or more items in a series if any of the items already contain commas.** Staff meetings were held on Thursday, May 7; Monday, June 7; and Friday, June 12. **Note:** Be sure to insert the semicolon *between* (not within) the items in a series.

Reference Manual

RULE 13
- number
(L. 57)

Hyphenate compound numbers between twenty-one and ninety-nine and fractions that are expressed as words.

Twenty-nine recommendations were approved by at least three-fourths of the members.

RULE 14
- compound adjective
(L. 67)

Hyphenate compound adjectives that come before a noun (unless the first word is an adverb ending in _–ly_).

We reviewed an up-to-date report on Wednesday.

But: The report was up to date.

But: We reviewed the highly rated report.

Note: A compound adjective is two or more words that function as a unit to describe a noun.

APOSTROPHES

RULE 15
' singular noun
(L. 37)

Use _'s_ to form the possessive of singular nouns.

The hurricane's force caused major damage to North Carolina's coastline.

RULE 16
' plural noun
(L. 37)

Use only an apostrophe to form the possessive of plural nouns that end in _s_.

The investors' goals were outlined in the stockholders' report.

But: The investors outlined their goals in the report to the stockholders.

But: The women's and children's clothing was on sale.

RULE 17
' pronoun
(L. 37)

Use _'s_ to form the possessive of indefinite pronouns (such as _someone's_ or _anybody's_); do not use an apostrophe with personal pronouns (such as _hers, his, its, ours, theirs,_ and _yours_).

She could select anybody's paper for a sample.

It's time to put the file back into its cabinet.

COLONS

RULE 18 ▶
: explanatory material
(L. 91)

Use a colon to introduce explanatory material that follows an independent clause.

The computer satisfies three criteria: speed, cost, and power.

But: The computer satisfies the three criteria of speed, cost, and power.

Remember this: only one coupon is allowed per customer.

Note: An independent clause can stand alone as a complete sentence. Do not capitalize the word following the colon.

PERIODS

RULE 19 ▶
. polite request
(L. 91)

Use a period to end a sentence that is a polite request.

Will you please call me if I can be of further assistance.

Note: Consider a sentence a polite request if you expect the reader to respond by doing as you ask rather than by giving a yes-or-no answer.

QUOTATION MARKS

RULE 20 ▶
" quotation
(L. 41)

Use quotation marks around a direct quotation.

Harrison responded by saying, "Their decision does not affect us."

But: Harrison responded by saying that their decision does not affect us.

RULE 21 ▶
" title
(L. 41)

Use quotation marks around the title of a newspaper or magazine article, chapter in a book, report, and similar terms.

The most helpful article I found was "Multimedia for All."

ITALICS (OR UNDERLINE)

RULE 22 ▶
title
(L. 41)

Italicize (or underline) the titles of books, magazines, newspapers, and other complete published works.

Grisham's *The Brethren* was reviewed in a recent *USA Today* article.

GRAMMAR

SENTENCES

RULE 23 ▶
fragment
(L. 21)

Avoid sentence fragments.

> *Not:* She had always wanted to be a financial manager. But had not had the needed education.

> *But:* She had always wanted to be a financial manager but had not had the needed education.

Note: A fragment is a part of a sentence that is incorrectly punctuated as a complete sentence. In the first sentence above, "but had not had the needed education" is not a complete sentence because it does not contain a subject.

RULE 24 ▶
run-on
(L. 21)

Avoid run-on sentences.

> *Not:* Mohamed is a competent worker he has even passed the MOUS exam.

> *Not:* Mohamed is a competent worker, he has even passed the MOUS exam.

> *But:* Mohamed is a competent worker; he has even passed the MOUS exam.

> *Or:* Mohamed is a competent worker. He has even passed the MOUS exam.

Note: A run-on sentence is two independent clauses that run together without any punctuation between them or with only a comma between them.

AGREEMENT

RULE 25 ▶
agreement singular
agreement plural
(L. 67)

Use singular verbs and pronouns with singular subjects; use plural verbs and pronouns with plural subjects.

> I was happy with my performance.

> Janet and Phoenix were happy with their performance.

> Among the items discussed were our raises and benefits.

RULE 26 ▶
agreement pronoun
(L. 81)

Some pronouns *(anybody, each, either, everybody, everyone, much, neither, no one, nobody,* and *one)* are always singular and take a singular verb. Other pronouns *(all, any, more, most, none,* and *some)* may be singular or plural, depending on the noun to which they refer.

> Each of the employees has finished his or her task.

> Much remains to be done.

> Most of the pie was eaten, but most of the cookies were left.

RULE 27 ▶
agreement intervening words
(L. 81)

Disregard any intervening words that come between the subject and verb when establishing agreement.

> The box containing the books and pencils has not been found.

> Alex, accompanied by Tricia, is attending the conference and taking his computer.

RULE 28 ▶
agreement nearer noun
(L. 101)

If two subjects are joined by *or, either/or, neither/nor,* or *not only/but also,* make the verb agree with the subject nearer to the verb.

> Neither the coach nor the players are at home.

> Not only the coach but also the referee is at home.

> *But:* Both the coach and the referee are at home.

PRONOUNS

RULE 29 ►
nominative pronoun
(L. 107)

Use nominative pronouns (such as *I, he, she, we, they,* and *who*) as subjects of a sentence or clause.

> The programmer and <u>he</u> are reviewing the code.
>
> Barb is a person <u>who</u> can do the job.

RULE 30 ►
objective pronoun
(L. 107)

Use objective pronouns (such as *me, him, her, us, them,* and *whom*) as objects of a sentence, clause, or phrase.

> The code was reviewed by the programmer and <u>him</u>.
>
> Barb is the type of person <u>whom</u> we can trust.

ADJECTIVES AND ADVERBS

RULE 31 ►
adjective/adverb
(L. 101)

Use comparative adjectives and adverbs (*-er, more,* and *less*) when referring to two nouns or pronouns; use superlative adjectives and adverbs (*-est, most,* and *least*) when referring to more than two.

> The <u>shorter</u> of the <u>two</u> training sessions is the <u>more</u> helpful one.
>
> The <u>longest</u> of the <u>three</u> training sessions is the <u>least</u> helpful one.

WORD USAGE

RULE 32 ►
accept/except
(L. 117)

***Accept* means "to agree to"; *except* means "to leave out."**

> All employees <u>except</u> the maintenance staff should <u>accept</u> the agreement.

RULE 33 ►
affect/effect
(L. 117)

***Affect* is most often used as a verb meaning "to influence"; *effect* is most often used as a noun meaning "result."**

> The ruling will <u>affect</u> our domestic operations but will have no <u>effect</u> on our Asian operations.

RULE 34 ►
farther/further
(L. 117)

***Farther* refers to distance; *further* refers to extent or degree.**

> The <u>farther</u> we drove, the <u>further</u> agitated he became.

RULE 35 ►
personal/personnel
(L. 117)

***Personal* means "private"; *personnel* means "employees."**

> All <u>personnel</u> agreed not to use email for <u>personal</u> business.

RULE 36 ►
principal/ principle
(L. 117)

***Principal* means "primary"; *principle* means "rule."**

> The <u>principle</u> of fairness is our <u>principal</u> means of dealing with customers.

MECHANICS

CAPITALIZATION

RULE 37 ▶
≡ sentence
(L. 31)

Capitalize the first word of a sentence.

> Please prepare a summary of your activities.

RULE 38 ▶
≡ proper noun
(L. 31)

Capitalize proper nouns and adjectives derived from proper nouns.

> Judy Hendrix drove to Albuquerque in her new Pontiac convertible.

Note: A proper noun is the official name of a particular person, place, or thing.

RULE 39 ▶
≡ time
(L. 31)

Capitalize the names of the days of the week, months, holidays, and religious days (but do not capitalize the names of the seasons).

> On Thursday, November 25, we will celebrate Thanksgiving, the most popular holiday in the fall.

RULE 40 ▶
≡ noun #
(L. 77)

Capitalize nouns followed by a number or letter (except for the nouns *line, note, page, paragraph,* and *size*).

> Please read Chapter 5, which begins on page 94.

RULE 41 ▶
≡ compass point
(L. 77)

Capitalize compass points (such as *north, south,* or *northeast*) only when they designate definite regions.

> From Montana we drove south to reach the Southwest.

RULE 42 ▶
≡ organization
(L. 111)

Capitalize common organizational terms (such as *advertising department* and *finance committee*) only when they are the actual names of the units in the writer's own organization and when they are preceded by the word *the*..

> The report from the Advertising Department is due today.

> *But:* Our advertising department will submit its report today.

RULE 43 ▶
≡ course
(L. 111)

Capitalize the names of specific course titles but not the names of subjects or areas of study.

> I have enrolled in Accounting 201 and will also take a marketing course.

NUMBER EXPRESSION

RULE 44 ▶
general
(L. 41)

In general, spell out numbers zero through ten, and use figures for numbers above ten.

> We rented two movies for tonight.

> The decision was reached after 27 precincts sent in their results.

RULE 45 ▶
figure
(L. 41)

Use figures for

- **Dates. (Use *st, d,* or *th* only if the day comes before the month.)**

  The tax report is due on April 15 *(not* April 15<u>th</u>)

  We will drive to the camp on the 23d (or *23rd* or *23rd*) of May.

- **All numbers if two or more *related* numbers both above and below ten are used in the same sentence.**

  Mr. Carter sent in 7 receipts, and Ms. Cantrell sent in 22.

  But: The 13 accountants owned three computers each.

- **Measurements (time, money, distance, weight, and percent).**

  The $500 statue we delivered at 7 a.m. weighed 6 pounds.

- **Mixed numbers.**

  Our sales are up 9½ (or *9 1/2*) percent over last year.

RULE 46 ▶
word
(L. 57)

Spell out

- **A number used as the first word of a sentence.**

  Seventy-five people attended the conference in San Diego.

- **The shorter of two adjacent numbers.**

  We have ordered 3 two-pound cakes and one 5 pound cake for the reception.

- **The words *million* and *billion* in even amounts (do not use decimals with even amounts).**

  A $5 ticket can win $28 million in this month's lottery.

- **Fractions.**

  Almost one-half of the audience responded to the question.

Note: When fractions and the numbers twenty-one through ninety-nine are spelled out, they should be hyphenated.

ABBREVIATIONS

RULE 47 ▶
abbreviate none
(L. 67)

In general business writing, do not abbreviate common words (such as *dept.* or *pkg.*), compass points, units of measure, or the names of months, days of the week, cities, or states (except in addresses).

  Almost one-half of the audience indicated they were at least 5 feet 8 inches tall.

Note: Do not insert a comma between the parts of a single measurement.

RULE 48 ▶
abbreviate measure
(L. 87)

In technical writing, on forms, and in tables, abbreviate units of measure when they occur frequently. Do not use periods.

  14 oz   5 ft 10 in   50 mph   2 yrs 10 mo

RULE 49 ▶
abbreviate lowercase
(L. 87)

In most lowercase abbreviations made up of single initials, use a period after each initial but no internal spaces.

  a.m.   p.m.   i.e.   e.g.   e.o.m.

  Exceptions: mph   mpg   wpm

RULE 50 ▶
abbreviate ≡
(L. 87)

In most all-capital abbreviations made up of single initials, do not use periods or internal spaces.

  OSHA   PBS   NBEA   WWW   VCR   MBA

  Exceptions: U.S.A.   A.A.   B.S.   Ph.D.   P.O.   B.C.   A.D.

GETTING STARTED

Introduction

Microsoft® Word for Windows is a word processing program that lets you create anything from a half-page memo to a 300-page report complete with charts, tables, and artwork. Naturally, a program this powerful requires some training in order to learn how to use its many features.

The *Gregg College Keyboarding & Document Processing Manual for Microsoft Word 2002* shows you step-by-step how to perform the tasks needed to create attractive business documents. Using this manual in conjunction with your textbook will enable you to develop the keyboarding and document processing skills needed for success in the contemporary business office.

This manual will also serve as a handy, permanent reference for reviewing the features of Word that you will use most often.

FORMAT OF THIS MANUAL

The major word processing tasks are presented in the pages that follow, along with step-by-step directions for completing each task. You will be able to follow the steps easily if you remember these signals (illustrated in the left margin) used throughout the manual:

Example: Move the insertion point to the beginning of page 2.

Choose Insert.

Press SHIFT+F12.

Press F7, ENTER.

- Numbered steps provide the exact instructions necessary for completing each task.

- The computer icon (symbol) indicates a hands-on activity that you should complete at your computer. All hands-on activities are screened in color so that you can easily identify them.

- Menu choices are shown in initial caps, with the keyboard-shortcut letter underlined and in bold.

- When key combinations are joined by a plus (+), press and hold down the first key while you press the second key; then release both keys.

- When key combinations are joined by a comma (,), press and release the first key, and then press and release the second key.

(continued on next page)

Center the title Agenda.

Open the file named *practice-21*.

Save the file with the new file name *student-21a*.

All directions in this manual apply to a right-handed mouse. If your mouse has been reset to accommodate a left-handed operator, your directions will differ.

- Words or characters that you are to type (Agenda in the example) are shown in a different font.

- The disk icon identifies instructions that apply only when you are using the correlated software that comes with your text. Check with your instructor or lab supervisor if you have questions.

- Two types of file names (shown in italic) are used in this manual. Those files named *practice-* are files that come with the correlated software. Those files named *student-* are files that you've worked on and saved.

- The "Go To" icon is a reminder to return to your textbook to complete the document processing exercises for the lesson.

In addition to these signals, note the meanings of the following terms that are common to all Windows programs:

- *Point* means to move the mouse until the mouse pointer on the screen is resting on the desired item.

- *Click* means to point to an item; then press and quickly release the left mouse button without moving the mouse.

- *Double-click* means to point to an item; then press and quickly release the left mouse button twice—without moving the mouse.

- *Drag* means to point to an item; then hold down the left mouse button while moving the mouse.

- *Right-click* means to point to an item; then press and quickly release the right mouse button.

WINDOWS HELP

Use the Windows' built-in Help to become familiar with Windows.

PRACTICE

To use Windows' built-in Help system to become familiar with Windows:

1. If you have not done so, turn on your computer and start Windows. Your screen should look similar to (but not necessarily exactly like) the following screen.

(continued on next page)

Click the Start button.

2. Click the Start button at the bottom left of your screen.
Note: Remember that to *click* means to move the mouse until the mouse pointer on the screen is resting on an item; then press and quickly release the left mouse button without moving the mouse.

(continued on next page)

3. When the Start menu appears, click **H**elp.

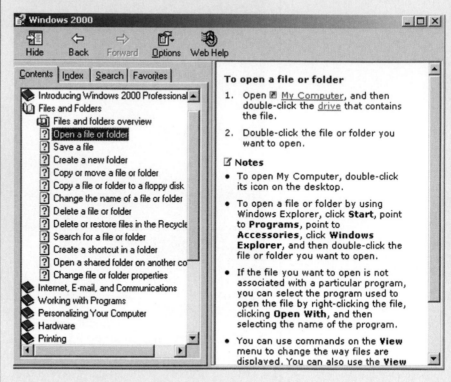

4. With the **C**ontents tab forward, select a topic you would like help on. The right window pane displays helpful step-by-step instructions related to the topic.

5. Click the Search tab.

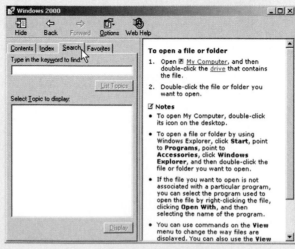

(continued on next page)

6. Type in a word processing related topic you would like help with.

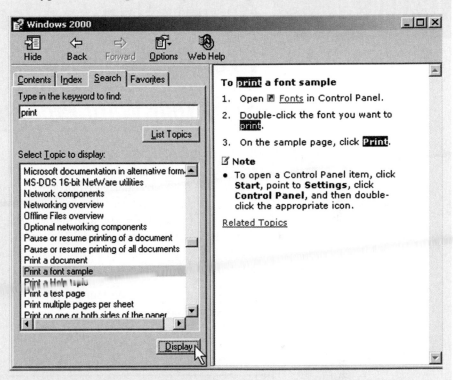

7. Click **L**ist Topics. Select a topic.

8. Select **D**isplay.

9. The help topic listed can be printed or simply read on screen.

10. Explore the Help window by choosing to display different topics.

11. When you finish exploring the Help window, click the Close button at the far right of the title bar to return to the Windows desktop.

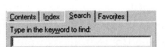

Type a keyword in the Search box to find information quickly.

Close button

Orientation to Word Processing—A

Start Your Word Processor

Before you can begin typing and formatting documents, you must be in your word processing program (in this case, Microsoft® Word 2002 for Windows). To access the word processor from the *Gregg College Keyboarding & Document Processing* software (referred to as GDP from this point on), click the Forward arrow whenever the screen prompts you to do so. The GDP program will automatically launch you into Microsoft Word. If necessary, you can also start Word from the GDP software through the file menu.

Note: For instructions on starting Microsoft Word from Windows, see the Appendix.

PRACTICE

Reminder: Complete these steps while at your computer.

1. Click Forward on your GDP screen to start Word.

In a few seconds, a Word blank document screen appears, ready for your input. (If you see a *Tip of the Day,* read the tip; then press Enter to close the box.)

The appearance of the screen depends on the default settings for your program. Your screen should look similar to the one below:

Title bar
Menu bar
Standard toolbar
Formatting toolbar
Ruler

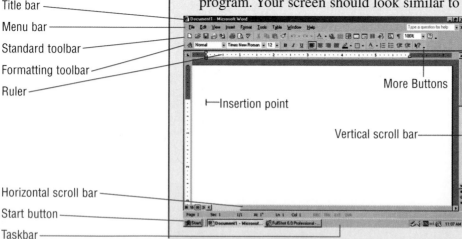

More Buttons

Insertion point

Vertical scroll bar

Horizontal scroll bar
Start button
Taskbar

(continued on next page)

2. The mouse pointer shows the location of items on the screen. The pointer takes on different shapes, depending on where it is positioned on the screen and the task on which you are working. With the mouse, point to each of these items on your screen:

- *Title bar:* Displays the name of the application program you're running (Microsoft Word) and the name of the current document (until documents have been saved, Word identifies them as *Document1, Document2,* and so on).

- *Menu bar:* Displays the list of choices available.

- *Standard toolbar:* Displays buttons that you can click with the mouse to perform common tasks. Click the More Buttons button to display additional buttons.

- *Formatting toolbar:* Displays information about formats and about buttons you can click to change formats. Click the More Buttons button to display additional buttons.

- *Ruler:* Shows the page margins, tabs, and indentions.

- *Insertion point:* Shows where text will appear when you type.

- *End-of-document marker:* Shows the position of the last character in your document.

- *Scroll bars:* Are used to display parts of the document that are not currently visible.

- *Status bar:* Displays information about your document and the position of the insertion point.

- *Start button:* Displays a menu that contains basic commands and features for Windows.

- *Taskbar:* Contains a button representing each program or Word document that is open.

Note: The toolbars show only buttons used most recently; many other buttons are available. To look for a button not shown on the docked tool bars, click the More Buttons button at the end of the toolbars. When a button is used that is not displayed on the toolbars, Word moves that button to the docked toolbars.

(continued on next page)

Choose a Command

A command tells Word what to do. For example, you can choose a command to tell Word to print a document, check your spelling, or create a table. You can choose commands in a variety of ways: from the toolbar, from the menu, or from the keyboard (using shortcut keys). An explanation of each method follows.

FROM THE TOOLBAR

Toolbars contain buttons that enable you to quickly choose frequently used commands. Word displays both a Standard and a Formatting toolbar.

To find out what each button does, point to the button. A message (called a ScreenTip) appears next to the button to identify it.

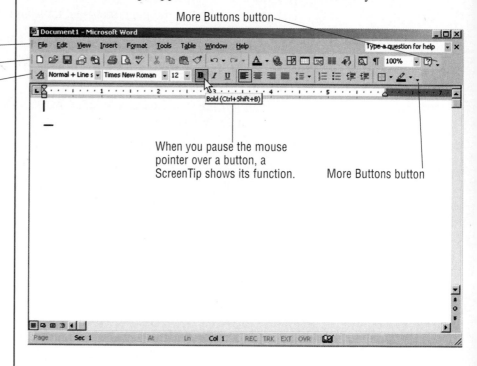

More Buttons button

Menu bar
Standard toolbar
Formatting toolbar

When you pause the mouse pointer over a button, a ScreenTip shows its function.

More Buttons button

(continued on next page)

Toolbar Options button

PRACTICE

Point to each button on the toolbar and read the ScreenTip.

Note: Although you will soon learn the purpose of each button, you can always pause the pointer over a button to see its function.

Note: Click the Toolbar Options button on the toolbars to add or remove buttons on the toolbar.

FROM THE MENU

Commands are grouped into the categories shown on the menu bar. When you choose a command from the menu bar, a drop-down menu opens that lists the specific commands available. For example, when you select **File**, the **File** drop-down menu appears.

Note: GDP will appear on the menu bar only when you open Word from within the GDP software.

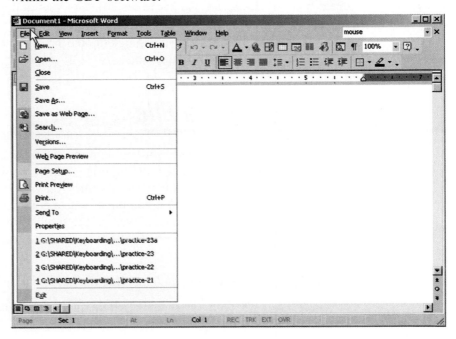

(continued on next page)

PRACTICE

Click the various menu items to view each drop-down menu and learn what options are available. Click in the blank area of the screen to close the drop-down menus or press ESC.

FROM THE KEYBOARD

Many commands can be executed using shortcut keys. These keys are listed on the menu to the right of the command. To choose commands using shortcut keys, simply press the appropriate shortcut key combinations. For example, to open the Print dialog box, press CTRL+P. Press ESC to close the dialog box or click cancel.

PRACTICE

1. Press CTRL+O to display the Open dialog box. Press ESC to close the dialog box.
2. Press SHIFT+F7 to display the Thesaurus dialog box. Press ESC to close the dialog box.

Open a File

When you start Word, a blank document is automatically opened so that you can begin typing immediately. To work on a document that you have previously saved (either on your data disk or on your computer's hard disk), you must issue a command to open that document file so it can be displayed on the screen. There are several ways to open a file.

Open button

1. To open a file:
   • From the toolbar, click the Open button.
   • From the menu, click the menu item **F**ile; then, on the drop-down menu, click **O**pen.

Note: When you choose **F**ile from the menu, the names of the last four documents you opened are displayed near the bottom of the drop-down menu. To quickly open one of these four documents, select (click) the document name.

(continued on next page)

To open a file you've worked on recently, choose it from the bottom of the File menu.

• On the keyboard (shortcut keys), press CTRL+O.

Select the method of choosing a command that you find most convenient. Each method accomplishes the same thing.

When you choose the Open command, a dialog box similar to the following appears (yours will differ, depending upon the files saved on your disk):

Click here to display the contents of a different drive.

If the folder or file you want to open is displayed, double-click to open it.

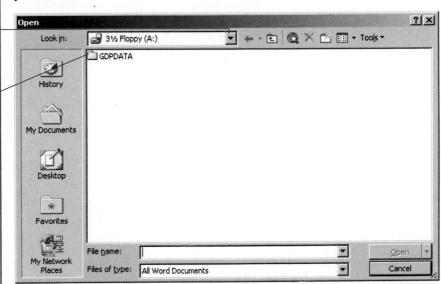

Note: Your list of drives and their contents will be different from those shown here.

(continued on next page)

2. If the folder or file you want to open is listed, double-click that folder or file name. If, however, you want to open a file that is on a disk in drive A, click anywhere in the Look **I**n box at the top of the Open dialog box to display a list of other file locations.

Double-click the drive that con-tains the file you want to open.

3. Click the icon for drive A.

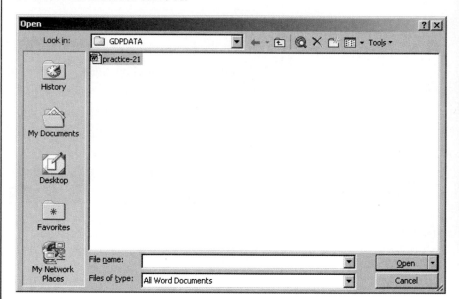

4. Select the file in drive A you want to open; then choose **O**pen (or double-click the file name).

Note: If the list of files on your data disk is too long to display all at once, you may have to scroll through the list until your file is visible.

PRACTICE

1. Open the file named *practice-21.*

The following document is displayed on your screen.

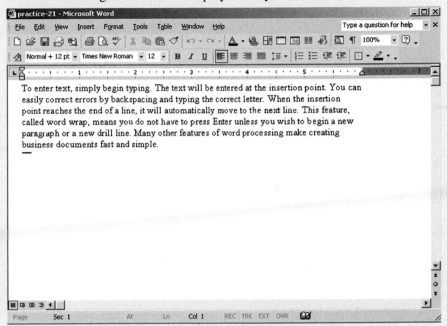

Quit Your Word Processor

To quit Word and return to the *Gregg College Keyboarding & Document Processing* program:

1. On the menu, choose **G**DP, **R**eturn to GDP.

If you have not saved your document, you will be prompted to save it. Once you choose **Y**es or **N**o, you will be returned to the GDP program.

Note: If you are not using the *Gregg College Keyboarding & Document Processing* program, see the instructions for quitting Microsoft Word in the Appendix.

(continued on next page)

PRACTICE

1. If necessary, open the file named *practice-21*.

2. Quit Word and return to GDP. Since you have not made any changes to the open document, you will not be asked if you want to save the changes. (If you accidentally made changes, choose **N**o.) You will be returned to the GDP program.

Lesson 22

Orientation to Word Processing—B

Navigate in a File

Do not confuse the insertion point with the mouse pointer (the mouse pointer is typically either an I-shaped symbol or an arrow that shows the location of the mouse on the screen).

The insertion point (a blinking vertical bar) shows where text will appear in the document as you type. If you want to insert text in another part of the document, you must first move the insertion point.

To move the insertion point to a different position in your document, do one of the following:

— Scroll box

— Scroll bar

To Navigate:	With the Mouse:	On the Keyboard:
Anywhere	Click where you want to position the insertion point.	Use the arrow keys to move to where you want to position the insertion point.
Through the document	Click the scroll bar (the area above or below the scroll box) to display the previous screen or to display the next screen.	Press PAGE UP to move backward through the document one screen at a time or PAGE DOWN to move forward through the document one screen at a time.
To the beginning or end of the line	Click at the beginning or end of the line.	Press HOME to move to the beginning of the line or END to move to the end of the line.
To the beginning or end of the document	Drag the scroll box to the top or bottom of the vertical scroll bar.	Press CTRL+HOME to move to the beginning of the document or CTRL+END to move to the end of the document.

Note: Using the scroll bar or scroll box does **not** move the insertion point. After navigating through text using the scroll bar or box, click in the text to move the insertion point.

(continued on next page)

Hands On

PRACTICE

1. Open the file named *practice-22*.

The following document is displayed on your screen.

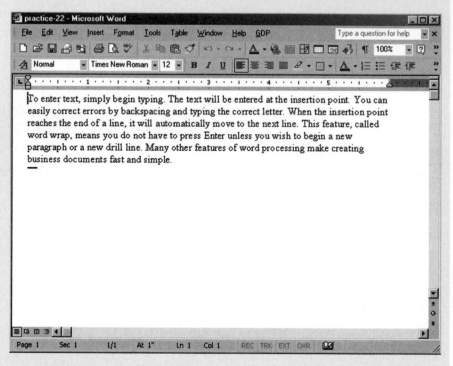

2. Locate the mouse pointer, the insertion point, and the end-of-document marker on the screen above and on your own computer screen. What do they mean?

3. Move the insertion point to the end of the document.

4. Move the insertion point immediately to the left of the "T" in "This" in line 3. What would happen if you were to press BACKSPACE now? What would happen if you were to press DELETE instead?

5. Move to the beginning of the same line (line 3).

6. Move to the beginning of the document.

Save a File

When you create a document, Word temporarily stores it in the computer's memory and assigns it a temporary name. However, if you quit

(continued on next page)

Word before saving the document to a disk or if you experience a power outage, your document can be lost.

To save a document permanently (so that you can open it and work on it again), you must save it either to your computer's hard disk or to your data disk. You don't have to wait until you finish a document to save it. To avoid accidental loss of data, save your work frequently.

To save a file for the first time:

On the menu, choose File, Save As.

The Save As dialog box displays, and you can name the file.

If necessary, select the drive where you want to save the document.

Type a name for the document.

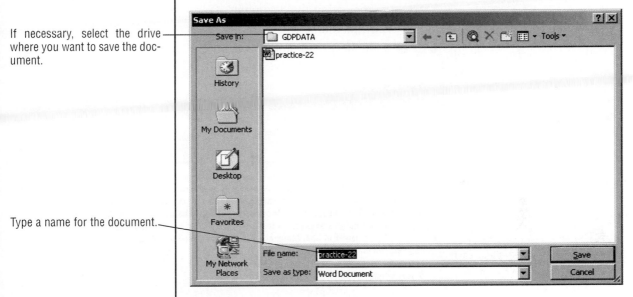

To save an existing document:

1. On the toolbar, click the Save button.

Or: On the menu, choose, File, Save.

Or: On the keyboard, press CTRL + S.

Save button

If you are using the correlated software, whenever you choose the Save command, a file name will be supplied automatically for all document processing activities in the textbook.

You must, however, name and save the practice activities in this manual.

Word assigns a temporary file name to each document you create, consisting of the first few words in the document. This temporary name is selected (highlighted). Type your preferred file name; the temporary name will be erased.

A file name can have up to 255 characters (including upper- and/or lowercase letters, numbers, spaces, and a few common symbols such as the hyphen or underline). In general, shorter file names are preferred because they are easier to display in Window's dialog boxes. Word automatically adds the extension *.doc* to your file name.

(continued on next page)

2. Choose OK.

Note: If you wish to save an existing file under a different name, from the menu choose **F**ile, Save **A**s. In the Save As dialog box, the existing document name will be highlighted. Type the new file name and choose OK. Choose Save **A**s if you want to make changes to a file but also want to save the original version.

PRACTICE

1. If necessary, open the file named *practice-22*.

2. Move to the end of the document.

3. Key your first and last name.

4. Choose the Save **A**s command from the File menu and save this file with the new file name *student-22*.

Your screen should now look like this.

Note that the file name has been changed to student-22.

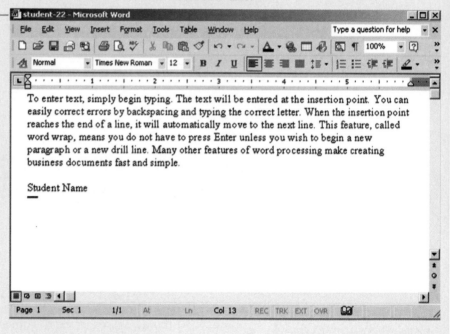

Close a File

To close the current document file and begin a new one immediately without quitting Word:

1. On the menu choose **F**ile, **C**lose.

(continued on next page)

Or: On the keyboard, press CTRL+F4.

Or: Click the Document Close button.

If it's a new document or an existing document to which you made changes, a dialog box appears asking if you want to save the document. To save your document or to save any changes, choose **Y**es. If more than one document is open, a dialog box will appear for each document. Choose **Y**es to save the document or any changes.

PRACTICE

1. If necessary, open the file named *practice-22*.
2. Move the insertion point to the top of the document and type today's date. Use the backspace key to correct any errors.
3. Press ENTER 2 times to leave 1 blank line after the date.
4. Close the document. When prompted to save changes, choose **N**o.

   Note: A red dotted line underlines the date. If a Smart tag Actions button appears on the screen, press ESC to clear.

New

When you start Word, a new blank document (named *Document1*) appears on the screen, ready for you to begin typing. When you finish that document and close it, a blank window appears, as shown.

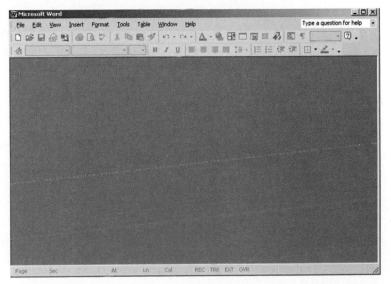

You cannot type in the blank window that appears when you close an open document.

(continued on next page)

To continue working, you must open either an existing document or create a new document.

To create a new document:

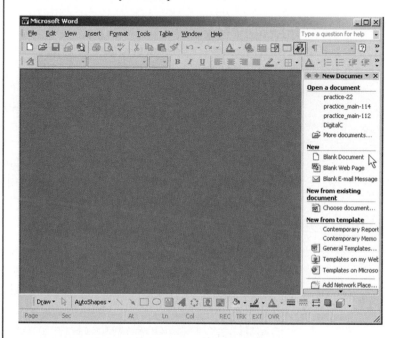

New button

1. On the toolbar, click the New button.

Or: On the menu, choose <u>F</u>ile, <u>N</u>ew. A New document task pane window appears to the right. Click Blank document under the heading New.
Or: On the keyboard, press CTRL+N.

Note: It is not necessary to close one document before opening another one. You can have numerous documents open at the same time and switch back and forth among them by choosing <u>W</u>indow on the menu bar and selecting the document you want from the list (or by pressing CTRL+F6).

PRACTICE

1. Create a new document and type your name and address.
2. Open the file named *practice-22*.
3. Choose <u>W</u>indow and switch to the other document.
4. Close the new file without saving it (as well as any other open files). Your screen should now show a blank window.

Lesson 23

Orientation to Word Processing—C

Select Text

To modify existing text, you must first select the text you want to change. You can then make any changes you wish: for example, you might want to change the selected text to italic or delete the text. Text that you select is highlighted—that is, the characters appear in reverse video, as shown in the following illustration:

The pointer is positioned in the Selection bar, the area immediately to the left of the text.

To enter text, simply begin typing
insertion point. You can easily cor
typing the correct letter. When the
line, it will automatically move to
word wrap, means you do not have
begin a new paragraph or a new dr

— Selected text is highlighted.

To select text using the mouse, do one of the following:

When you double-click to select a word, Word also selects the space after the word.

To Select:	Do This:
Any amount of text	Point and drag over the text you want to select.
A word	Double-click the word.
A line	Click in the Selection bar to the left of the line.
A sentence	Hold down CTRL and click anywhere in the sentence.
A paragraph	Double-click in the Selection bar next to the paragraph (*or* triple-click anywhere in the paragraph).
The entire document	Triple-click anywhere in the Selection bar (*or* press CTRL+A).

Note: To select any amount of text using the keyboard, first position the insertion point at the beginning of the text you want to select. Then hold down SHIFT and press the right and/or down arrow keys to extend the selection or click at the end of the selection.

(continued on next page)

If you accidentally select text, *deselect* the text (that is, cancel the operation) by clicking anywhere on the screen or by pressing any arrow key.

PRACTICE

1. If necessary, open the file named *practice-23*.

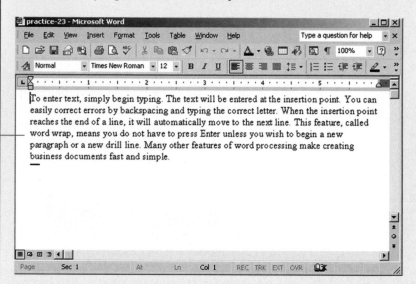

Selection bar —

2. Move the insertion point to the beginning of the document.

3. Press TAB to indent the first line of the paragraph. An AutoCorrect Options Box appears on the screen. Press ESC to cancel. Note that the word "You" moves to the second line.

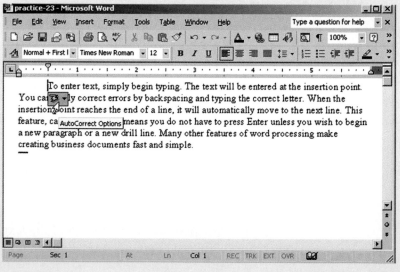

(continued on next page)

4. Select the word "automatically" in the third line by double-clicking anywhere in the word; then delete the word by pressing BACKSPACE.

5. Move the insertion point immediately to the left of "T" in "This" in line 3. Delete the space to the left by pressing BACKSPACE; then start a new paragraph at this point by pressing ENTER (to begin a new line). The line will automatically be indented.

6. Select the second paragraph by double-clicking in the Selection bar next to the paragraph or by triple-clicking anywhere in the paragraph.

7. Select the entire document by pressing CTRL+A. Now deselect the document by clicking anywhere on the screen or by pressing any arrow key. (When you press an arrow key, the text is no longer highlighted and the insertion point moves to the beginning or end of the document.)

8. Select the words "word processing" in the last sentence. In their place, type the words Microsoft Word for Windows.

   Your screen should now look like the following illustration:

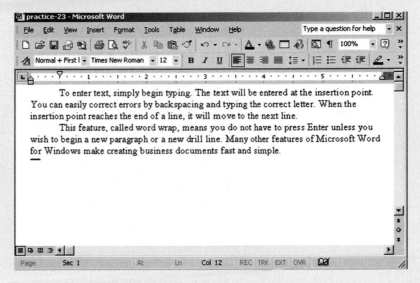

9. Close the file without saving your changes.

Bold

One way of making parts of a document (such as a report title) stand out is to format the text in bold. You can either bold text as you type or bold existing text.

To bold text as you type:

(continued on next page)

Bold button

This is bold
text.
This is not
bold.

Hands On

1. On the toolbar, click the Bold button. (The button appears outlined.)
   Or: On the keyboard, press CTRL+B.
2. Type the text you want to appear in bold.
3. Click the Bold button or press CTRL+B again to turn off bold.
The text appears on screen in bold.

To bold existing text:

1. Select the text you want to appear in bold.
2. Click the Bold button or press CTRL+B.

Note: The Bold command is a "toggle" command. Giving the command once turns Bold on; giving the command twice in succession turns it on and then off.

To remove bold formatting:

1. Select the text.
2. Click the Bold button or press CTRL+B again.

PRACTICE

1. Open the file named *practice-23a*.
2. Move to the end of the first paragraph. Space 1 time after the period, turn on bold, type `Amazing!`, and then turn off bold.
3. Select the words "word wrap" in line 4 and then bold them.
4. Remove the bold formatting from the word "`Amazing!`" in line 3.
5. In the last sentence, select and then bold "`Microsoft Word for Windows.`"
   Your screen should now look like this:

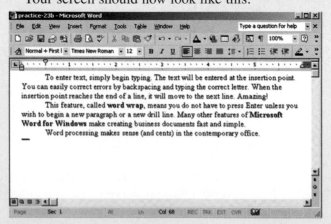

6. Close the file without saving your changes.

(continued on next page)

Undo/Redo a Command

To cancel a command before it has been executed or to deselect text, press ESC, click elsewhere on the screen, or press any arrow key. Once a command has been executed and you realize you made a mistake, you can usually reverse the last several actions.

UNDO A COMMAND

Undo button

To undo a command:

1. On the toolbar, click the Undo button. If you want to undo an action other than the most recent one, click the arrow to the right of the Undo button. Clicking the arrow will display a list of actions with the most recent action at the top. Select and click the actions you want to undo.

Or: On the menu, choose **E**dit. The drop-down menu displays the type of action you can reverse; for example, if the last action you performed was to cut a selection of text, the command is **U**ndo Cut. If you have been entering text, the command is **U**ndo Typing.

REDO A COMMAND

Redo button

To redo a command:

1. If you change your mind *again* and want to redo the command you just reversed, click the Redo button or choose **E**dit, **R**epeat.

PRACTICE

1. Open the file named *practice-23b*.
2. Move the insertion point to the end of the document (after the word "simple.").
3. Press ENTER to begin a new paragraph.
4. Type this sentence: Word processing makes sense (and cents) in the contemporary office.
5. Use the Undo command to undo (erase) the sentence you just typed.
6. Use the Redo command to reinsert the sentence.
   Your screen should now look like this:

(continued on next page)

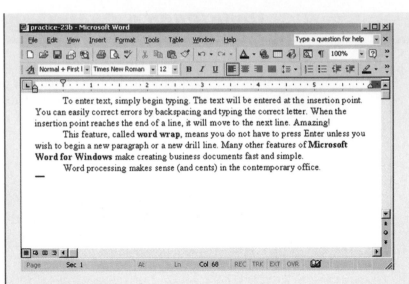

To enter text, simply begin typing. The text will be entered at the insertion point. You can easily correct errors by backspacing and typing the correct letter. When the insertion point reaches the end of a line, it will move to the next line. Amazing!

This feature, called **word wrap**, means you do not have to press Enter unless you wish to begin a new paragraph or a new drill line. Many other features of **Microsoft Word for Windows** make creating business documents fast and simple.

Word processing makes sense (and cents) in the contemporary office.

7. Close the file without saving your changes.

Help

Word's extensive on-line Help system contains all the information you need to use Word. Help is available in many places throughout the program and in a variety of formats. The most common uses of online Help are either to learn what something displayed on the screen means or to look up information in the online index.

PRACTICE

The Office Assistant anticipates the type of help you need and will suggest help topics based on your work. The Office Assistant also provides tips, visual examples, and detailed instructions for specific tasks to help you use Word more efficiently.

1. On the toolbar, click the Microsoft Word Help button.

Or: On the keyboard, press F1.

Microsoft Word Help button

2. Type a question in the space provided, then click Search.

Note: The Office Assistant may automatically appear to display tips depending on the task you are doing.

3. To hide the Office Assistant temporarily, on the menu, choose **H**elp, Hide the **O**ffice Assistant.

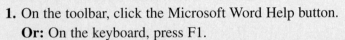

(continued on next page)

To turn off the Office Assistant for an entire Word session, click **O**ptions in the Office Assistant balloon. Then clear the **U**se the Office Assistant check box.

To find out what an option in a dialog box means:

Help button

1. Click the question mark button at the top right of the dialog box's title bar.

2. When the pointer turns into a question mark, drag the question mark to the option you want information about, and click the option. (For example, open the Print dialog box. Click the question mark on the title bar; then click on Curr**e**nt Page to see what it means.)

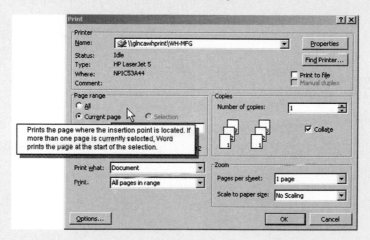

Note: Office Assistant must be turned off.

3. Press ESC twice to return to your document window.

(continued on next page)

To look up information in the online index:

1. On the menu, choose **H**elp, Microsoft Word **H**elp.

2. If necessary, click the **I**ndex tab.

3. Either type an entry or browse through the list of index topics and select one.

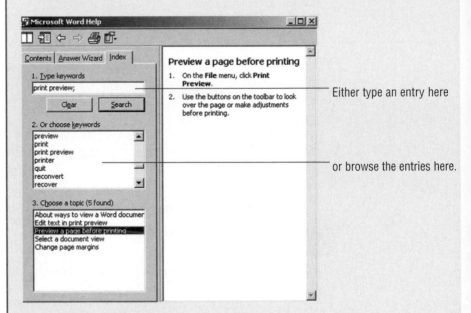

Either type an entry here

or browse the entries here.

4. Click **S**earch; Word will either display a Help window about the topic or display a list of related options from which to choose. (Occasionally, Word will display an Answer Wizard instead that guides you through the process; just follow the on-screen directions.)

5. To close a Help window, click the Close button.

6. Return to GDP.

Go To

Textbook

Orientation to Word Processing—D

Preview Pages Before Printing

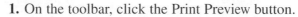

Use the Print Pre<u>v</u>iew command to see how your document will look when printed.

To preview a document before printing:

Print Preview Button

1. On the toolbar, click the Print Preview button.
   Or: On the menu, choose <u>F</u>ile, Print Pre<u>v</u>iew.
   Or: On the keyboard, press CTRL | F2.
   Your formatted document appears as a full page in the Preview Window, and a special Print Preview toolbar appears below the Menu bar.

Magnifying glass pointer

2. Move the mouse pointer onto the document. The pointer turns into a magnifying glass icon. Click anywhere in the document to view a magnified portion of the document; click again to return to the original magnification.

3. Click the Magnifier button on the Print Preview toolbar to change the mouse pointer back to its normal status. Now you can edit the document (although it may be difficult because of its size).

4. Click the <u>C</u>lose button on the Print Preview toolbar to return to the normal document window.

(continued on next page)

Magnifier

Close Button

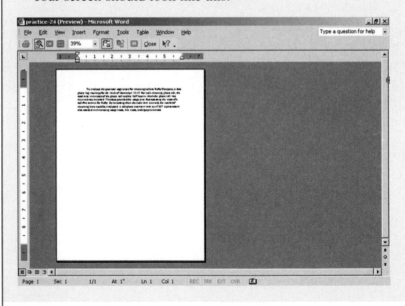

PRACTICE

1. Open the file named *practice-24.*

2. Choose Print Preview.

Your screen should look like this:

(continued on next page)

3. Move the mouse pointer anywhere in the document and click to see a magnified view; click again to return to normal magnification.

4. Click the **C**lose button to return to the normal document window.

Check Spelling and Grammar

Word's spelling and grammar tool checks your document for spelling, grammar, and typographical errors. When automatic spelling and grammar checking is active, spelling and grammar are checked as you type. Word marks possible spelling errors with a red wavy line and possible grammar errors with a green wavy line. To correct the errors immediately, click on the marked words with the right mouse button to display a list of suggested spellings or corrections; then choose from the list.

Note: To activate the grammar checker, click **C**heck grammar in the Spelling and Grammar dialog box.

To manually check spelling and grammar:

1. On the toolbar, click the Spelling and Grammar button.

Or: On the menu, choose **T**ools, **S**pelling and Grammar.

Or: On the keyboard, press F7.

Word scrolls through the document. If the program finds a problem, it displays the Spelling and Grammar dialog box.

Spelling and Grammar button

To check only part of a document, first select the passage to be checked and then choose the Spelling command.

Select the correct word from the list in the Suggestio**n**s box; then choose Change.

This box must be checked to activate the grammar checker.

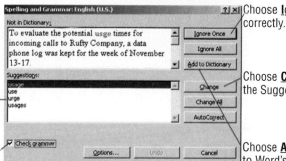

Choose **I**gnore if the word is spelled correctly.

Choose **C**hange to accept the spelling in the Suggestio**n**s box.

Choose **A**dd to add the word to Word's custom dictionary.

2. Each time the program stops for a spelling error, do one of the following:

• If a word in the Suggestio**n**s list is the correct spelling, select that word, and then choose **C**hange.

(continued on next page)

- If the word in the Not in Dictionary box is spelled correctly, choose **I**gnore Once (or **I**gnore All if you want the speller to ignore all occurrences of this word in your document).

  Note: If you want to add this word to the custom dictionary, choose **A**dd to Dictionary.

- If the correct word is not displayed in the Suggesti**o**ns list, click on the highlighted word in the Not in Dictionary box, type the correction, then choose **C**hange.

3. Each time the program stops for a grammar error, do one of the following:

- Compare the description of the error with the suggested correction in the Suggestions box.
- If the change is appropriate, choose **C**hange.
- If the change is not appropriate, choose **I**gnore Once or **I**gnore All.

4. When the dialog box appears with the message "The spelling and grammar check is complete," choose OK.

Note: Word will automatically correct some typical mistakes immediately after you type them—often without you being aware of it. For example, if you type "teh," Word will automatically change it to "the" on the fly (try it).

To see which words will be automatically corrected, on the menu, choose **T**ools, **A**utoCorrect Options. Be sure the AutoCorrect tab is active.

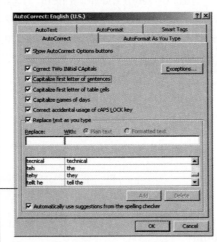

You can add to or delete items from this list as desired.

Even the spelling checker, however, will not identify omitted words, misused words, or typographical errors that form a new word (such as "sing" for "sign"). Thus, you should always proofread your documents manually before submitting them.

(continued on next page)

Once you spell check a document or choose **I**gnore, errors will no longer be marked, even if you spell check the document again.

These misstrokes are automatically corrected as soon as you press the space bar.

PRACTICE

1. If necessary, open the file named *practice-24*.

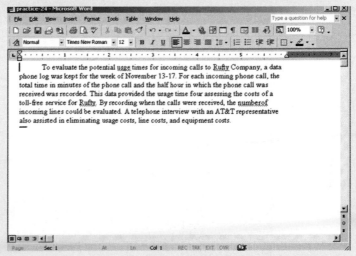

2. Choose the **S**pelling and Grammar command.

   a. Word displays the word "usge" in the Not in Dictionary box and suggests the word "usage" instead. Choose **C**hange to accept this suggestion.

   b. Word displays "Rufty" in the Not in Dictionary box and suggests the word "Rutty" instead. However, the word "Rufty" is correct, and it occurs throughout the document. Choose I**g**nore All so that Word will not flag this word again. Instead of choosing I**g**nore All, you could choose **A**dd to add the word to Word's custom dictionary.

   c. Word displays "numberof" in the Not in Dictionary box and provides a suggested spelling. Choose the correct suggestion. Then choose **C**hange.

   d. When Word displays the dialog box with the message "The spelling and grammar check is complete," choose OK.

   e. Manually proofread the document after running the speller. Note that one error has not been corrected. In line 4, the word "four" should be "for." Because "four" is in Word's internal dictionary, it was not flagged. Change "four" to "for."

Your screen should now look like the following illustration:

(continued on next page)

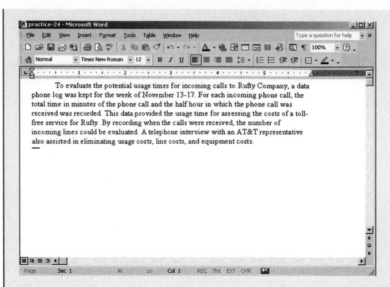

3. Save the document with the file name *student-24*; then close the file.

Show Formatting

When you press a nonprinting key such as TAB or ENTER, Word inserts a formatting mark into the document. For example, pressing ENTER inserts a paragraph mark (¶) and starts a new paragraph. Word defines a paragraph as any text or graphic that is followed by a ¶ mark.

To see exactly where a paragraph ends or how many spaces you inserted, display the formatting marks.

To view formatting marks on the screen:

1. On the toolbar, click the Show/Hide ¶ button (if displayed).

Show/Hide ¶ button

Or: On the menu, choose **T**ools, **O**ptions; select the View tab; choose **A**ll under Formatting marks; then choose OK.

Or: On the keyboard, press CTRL + SHIFT + 8.

The document now displays all of the formatting marks. Even though the formatting marks are displayed on the screen, they will not appear on the printed document.

(continued on next page)

Space character (•) ⎯⎯⎯⎯⎯⎯⎯⎯

Paragraph mark (¶) ⎯⎯⎯⎯⎯⎯⎯⎯

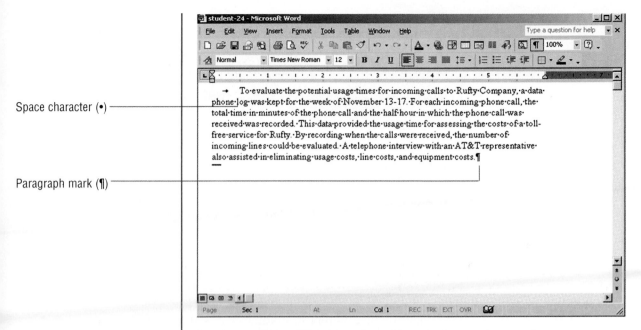

2. Choose Show/Hide ¶ again to hide the formatting marks.

To view format settings for a paragraph, choose **H**elp, What's **T**his?

Or: On the keyboard, press SHIFT+F1.

The mouse pointer contains a question mark.

Click the text you want to check. A Reveal formatting task pane window opens on the right of your screen. Close the take pane when finished.

(continued on next page)

Hands On

PRACTICE

1. If necessary, open the file named *student-24*.
2. Choose Show/Hide ¶ to display the formatting marks.

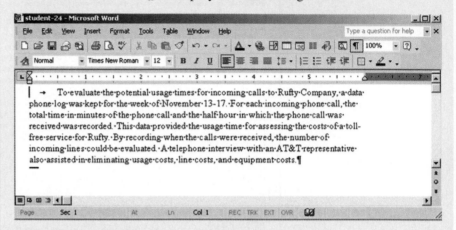

3. Identify the different formatting marks shown on the screen. What does the mark "•" indicate?
4. Choose Show/Hide ¶ again to hide the formatting marks.
5. Select the text 'November 13-17' and apply bold formatting.
6. Press Shift+F1 and click the bold text.

What's This pointer

7. Read the information in the Task Pane Window on the right of your screen.

(continued on next page)

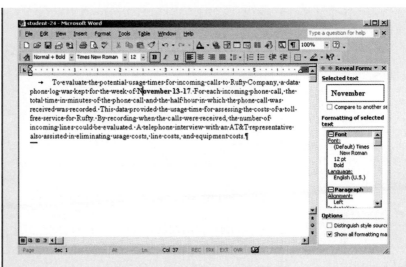

8. Close the Task Pane Window.

Print

It is always a good idea to save a document before printing it. That way, if your printer causes a problem, you will not lose any of your work.

To print the document displayed on the screen:

Print button

1. On the toolbar, click the Print button. (Clicking the Print button prints the entire document immediately, thereby skipping steps 2–3 below. If you want to change printers or print only a portion of a document, access Print through the **F**ile menu.)

Or: On the menu, choose **F**ile, **P**rint.

Or: On the keyboard, press CTRL+P.

2. If you choose Print from the menu or use the shortcut keys, select the print options you want from the Print dialog box. (To print one copy of the entire document, you will not need to make any changes.)

(continued on next page)

Select Current page to print just the page containing the insertion point.

Enter the page range if you want to print only certain pages (for example, typing "2–4" would cause pages 2 through 4 of a document to print).

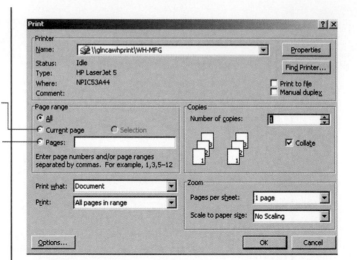

3. Choose OK.

Note: If you want to print only a part of a document, first select the part you want to print, choose the Print command, and choose Selection under Page range.

PRACTICE

1. If necessary, open the file named *student-24*.

2. Print two copies of this document.

3. Return to GDP.

Email Basics

Email a Document

The email feature in Word enables you to email the current active document or open an existing Word document to send as an email.

To send the document in the active window as an email message:

E-mail button

1. On the toolbar, click the E-mail button.

Or: On the menu, choose **F**ile, Sen**d** To, **M**ail Recipient.

The email header displays and your document appears as the email message.

2. Type the recipient name(s) in the **To** text box. Separate multiple names with semicolons.

3. By default, the document's name appears in the **Subject** box. If you want, you can type your own subject name. Type the subject of the email in the **Subject** text box.

4. Click **S**end a Copy to email the document if instructed to do so.

Hands On

PRACTICE

1. Open a new document.

2. Type the following paragraphs as shown.

    Email has become the most convenient way to send a quick
    question or message to anyone who has access to an online
    service. The writer needs no paper, pen, envelope, or
    stamp. Best of all, the message is delivered much more
    rapidly in digital form than a hard copy can be carried
    by the U.S. Post Office.

    One of the most popular uses for email is the party
    invitation, which can include sound, animation, an
    attached guest list, a map with directions, and even a
    digital photo album. The guest has the opportunity to
    RSVP by email after, in some cases, peeking at the entire
    guest list and seeing who has accepted and who has
    declined the invitation.

(continued on next page)

3. Click the E-mail button on the Standard toolbar.

4. Type <Instructor's email address> in the **To** box.

5. Type Email Today in the **Subject** box.

6. Click **S**end a Copy to send the email if instructed to do so.

7. Save the file with the name *student-25*.

To email an existing document:

1. Open the document.

2. Click the E-mail button on the Standard toolbar.

3. Type the email address in the **To** box.

4. Check the **Subject** line. It should contain the name of the file.

5. Click **S**end a Copy to email the document if instructed to do so.

Note: It is also possible to email a document as an attachment.

Attach File button

1. Click the Attach File button.

2. Locate the file in the Insert Attachment dialog box and click **A**ttach. Change drive and folder if necessary.

Note: The file to be attached to the email message appears in the email header.

3. Return to GDP.

PRACTICE

1. Open *student-22*.
2. Click the E-mail button on the Standard toolbar.
3. Type <Teacher's email address> in the **To** box.
4. Check the **Subject** line. It should contain the name of the file.
5. Click the Attach File button.
6. Locate the file *student-24* in the Insert Attachment dialog box and click **A**ttach.
7. Click **S**end a Copy to email the document if instructed to do so.
8. Return to GDP.

One-Page Business Reports

Alignment

Word provides four ways of aligning text between the left and right margins:

Left alignment is the default setting.

- *Left:* Aligns text flush with the left margin, leaving an uneven right edge.

- *Right:* Aligns text flush with the right margin, leaving an uneven left edge.

- *Centered:* Centers the text between the left and right margins.

- *Justified:* Aligns text flush with both the left and right margins.

To change the alignment of text:

1. On the Formatting toolbar, click the desired alignment button.

Alignment buttons:

Align Center Align Justify
Left   Right

Or: On the menu, choose F**o**rmat, **P**aragraph.

- Click the down arrow in the Ali**g**nment box, and select the desired alignment. (Be sure the **I**ndents and Spacing tab is active.)

- Choose OK.

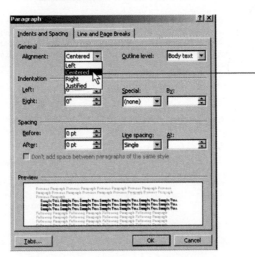

Alignment options

Or: On the keyboard, press:

- CTRL+L for left alignment.

- CTRL+E for center alignment.

(continued on next page)

- CTRL+R for right alignment.
- CTRL+J for justified alignment.

PRACTICE

1. Open the file named *practice-26*.
2. Be sure the insertion point is at the beginning of the document. Press ENTER 2 times; then move the insertion point back to the beginning of the document.
3. Type the word Draft.
4. Center the word DRAFT on the first line in all caps and bold.
5. In the first line of paragraph 1, change *"increased"* to "increase in the."
6. All paragraphs are now shown with left alignment. Change paragraph 2 to justified alignment.
7. Change paragraph 3 to right alignment.

   Your screen should now look like this:

Center alignment

Left alignment

Justified alignment

Right alignment

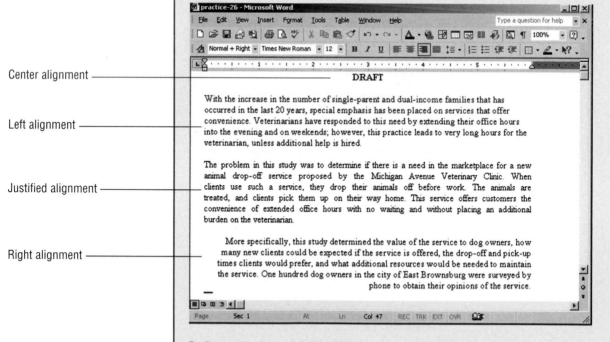

8. Save the file with the file name *student-26*.

(continued on next page)

Font Size

Font sizes are measured in *points*; 1 point (abbreviated *pt*) is equal to 1/72 of an inch. The point size refers to the height of a character. Thus, a 12-pt font is 1/6 inch in height.

Shown below are some examples of different font sizes you can use.

10-point Font Size

12-point Font Size

18-point Font Size

24-point Font Size

You can easily change the font size in your text. Avoid, however, using too many font sizes in the same document.

To change font size:

1. Position the insertion point where you want to begin using the new font size (or select the text you want to change).
2. On the Formatting toolbar, click the down arrow to the right of the Font Size box.
3. Choose the font size you want (scroll the list if necessary).

   Or: On the menu, choose F**o**rmat, **F**ont

   Or: On the keyboard, press CTRL+D.

Select the Font tab if it is not already active. When the Font dialog box appears, choose the font size you want; then choose OK.

Font Size

You can also change font size through the Font dialog box.

(continued on next page)

PRACTICE

1. Open a new document.
2. Center and type the following three lines.

   Your Name
   Your School
   Today's Date

3. Change the font size for the first line to 18 points.
4. Change the font size for the second line to 14 points.
5. Save your file with the file name *student-26b*.
6. Return to GDP.

Multipage Business Reports

Page Numbering

Use the Page Numbers command to insert the correct page number in the upper right corner of each page. You can use this same command to hide the page number on page 1 of the document.

If you are in Normal view (the default), you won't see the page numbers on your screen, but they will appear when the document is printed. To see page numbers on the screen, first switch to Print Layout View.

To switch to Print Layout View:

Click the Print Layout View button to the left of the horizontal scroll bars at the bottom of the window.

Or: On the menu, choose **V**iew, **P**rint Layout.

Print Layout View button

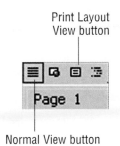

Page 1

Normal View button

To number pages:

1. On the menu, choose **I**nsert, Page N**u**mbers. The Page Numbers dialog box appears.

2. Click the down arrow in the **P**osition box and select Top of page (Header).

3. Click the down arrow in the **A**lignment box and choose Right, if necessary.

Clear this check box to hide the page number on page 1.

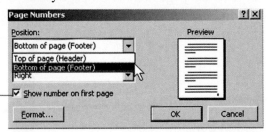

4. To suppress (hide) the page number on page 1 of your document, clear (deselect) the **S**how number on first page check box.

5. Click OK.

Note: To begin numbering pages with a number other than 1, in the Page Numbers dialog box, choose **F**ormat. In the Page Number Format dialog box, choose Start **a**t; then type the correct page number.

(continued on next page)

PRACTICE

1. Open the file named *practice-27*. (If necessary, switch to Print Layout View by clicking the Print Layout View button to the left of the horizontal bars or by choosing **V**iew, **P**rint Layout.)

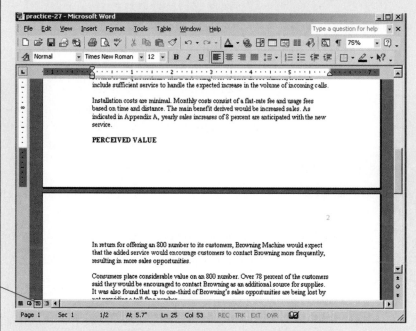

Print Layout View button

2. Use the Page Numbers command to automatically insert page numbers at the top right of each page.

3. Hide the page number on page 1.

4. Print the document to ensure that the page numbers are positioned correctly.

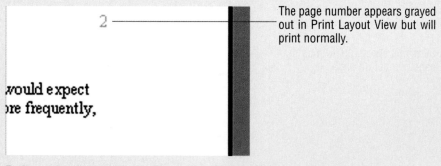

The page number appears grayed out in Print Layout View but will print normally.

5. Save the file with the file name *student-27a*.

(continued on next page)

Page Break

As you type, Word automatically starts a new page when the current page is filled. When you are in Normal view, the new page is indicated by a row of dots. This is called a *soft page break* because the page break can move, depending upon whether text is added to or deleted from the page. The status bar also changes to reflect which page of the document the insertion point is in.

Soft page break —

Normal View button —

The insertion point is currently — on page 2.

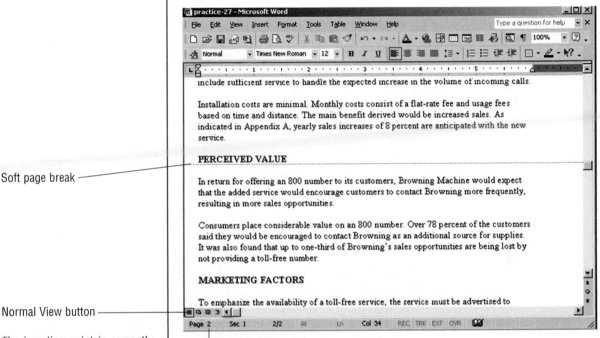

To force a page to end at a particular spot, you would insert a *hard page break.* No matter what text is added to or deleted from the document, the page will end at this point unless you later delete the page break.

To insert a hard page break:

1. Position the insertion point where you want the page to end.
2. On the menu, choose **I**nsert, **B**reak; select **P**age break; then click OK.
   Or: On the keyboard, press CTRL+ENTER.

In Normal View, a hard page break is indicated by a row of dots and the words *Page Break*. In Print Layout View, you will see two separate pages.

(continued on next page)

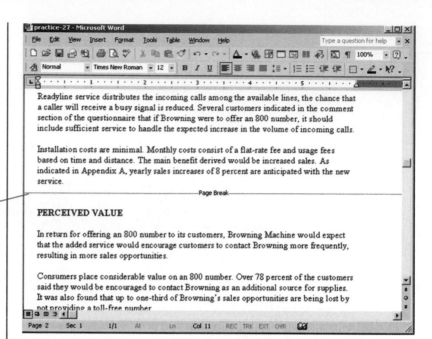

Hard page break—

Note: To remove a hard page break, select the page break and press BACKSPACE or DELETE.

PRACTICE

1. If necessary, open the file named *student-27a*.
2. Change to Normal View; then move the insertion point immediately in front of the side heading *PERCEIVED VALUE*.
3. Insert a hard page break.
4. Save the file with the file name *student-27b*.
5. Return to GDP.

Lesson 28

Bulleted and Numbered Lists

Bullets and Numbering

Numbering
button

Bullets
button

To call attention to a list of items, you might want to format them with bullets or with numbers. If the sequence of the items in the list is important, use numbers; if not, use bullets. The numbers or bullets are automatically indented from the left margin but may be repositioned, as you will see later.

To add bullets or numbers:

1. Position the insertion point where you want the bullets or numbers to begin.
2. Type your list of items. (Remember, if items in the list are multiline, insert a blank line between the items for readability.)

Note: If an indented paragraph immediately follows a list, type both the list **and** the indented paragraph **before** you apply bullets or numbers to ensure that a succeeding paragraph is indented correctly when you press TAB.

To insert a line break within a bulleted or numbered list (for example, to add a blank line or an explanatory note that begins on a separate line), press SHIFT+ENTER.

3. Select the lines to format with bullets or numbers.
4. On the Formatting toolbar, click either the Bullets or the Numbering button.

   Or: On the menu, choose Format, Bullets and Numbering; select the Bulleted tab or the Numbered tab; then select the bullet or numbering format you wish and click OK.
5. Click the Decrease Indent button.

DECREASE INDENT

Decrease Indent button

By default, Word indents a bulleted or numbered list. However, numbers and bullets should appear at the left margin in a document with blocked paragraphs. Use the Decrease Indent button on the Formatting toolbar to reposition lists at the left margin.

To position a list at the left margin:

1. Create the bulleted or numbered list as explained in Steps 1–4.
2. Select the list.

(continued on next page)

3. On the Formatting toolbar, click the Decrease Indent button to position the bullets or numbers at the left margin.

If you insert bullets or numbers by mistake, select the list of items again, and click the Bullets or Numbering button to delete them.

Please complete these jobs:	Please complete these jobs:	Please complete these jobs:
Order the mailroom supplies.	• Order the mailroom supplies.	1. Order the mailroom supplies.
Change the date of my next meeting to June 30.	• Change the date of my next meeting to June 30.	2. Change the date of my next meeting to June 30.
Update the cost spreadsheet.	• Update the cost spreadsheet.	3. Update the cost spreadsheet.
I would appreciate your giving me a call at 555-1036 when these tasks are finished.	I would appreciate your giving me a call at 555-1036 when these tasks are finished.	I would appreciate your giving me a call at 555-1036 when these tasks are finished.
Unformatted List	Bulleted List	Numbered List

PRACTICE

1. Open the file named *practice-28*.

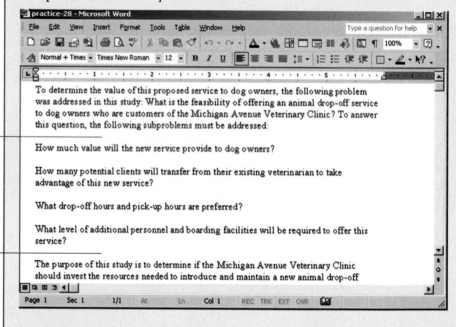

Convert to numbered list.

2. Format the sentences with question marks as a numbered list; then click the Decrease Indent button to position the numbered list at the left margin. (Remember to select the sentences.)

3. Move the insertion point to the end of the document (Hint: CTRL+END), and insert the following text:

(continued on next page)

Provide a better understanding of the need for this service in the marketplace.

Define some of the mechanics of the service.

Provide the needed direction on how to smoothly introduce this drop-off service if sufficient support is found.

Although cat owners also represent a large client base for the veterinarian, they were excluded from this study because cats do not have to be licensed.

4. Select the three sentences above the last paragraph and apply bullets to the list.
5. With the list still selected, click the Decrease Indent button to position the list at the left margin.
6. Choose Print Preview to see how your document will look when it is printed.

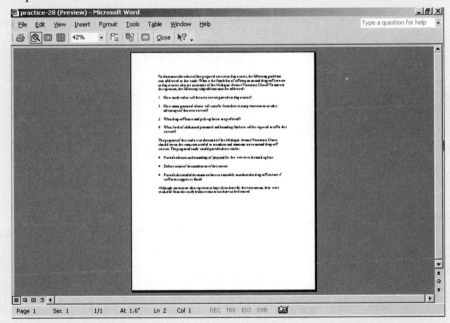

7. Save the file with the file name *student-28*.
8. Return to GDP.

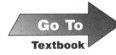
Go To
Textbook

Lesson 29

Academic Reports

Line Spacing

Single spacing is Word's default setting. You can easily change the line spacing from single to 1.5 line spacing (which adds an extra half line of space between typed lines) or to double-spacing (which adds an extra line of space between typed lines). The precise amount of space between lines is determined by the size of the font you are using.

To change line spacing:

1. Move the insertion point into the paragraph you want to change (or select the paragraphs you want to change).
2. On the menu, choose F**o**rmat, **P**aragraph; then select the **I**ndents and Spacing tab.
3. Click the down arrow in the Li**n**e spacing list box, and select the desired line spacing option.

Line spacing button

Line spacing options

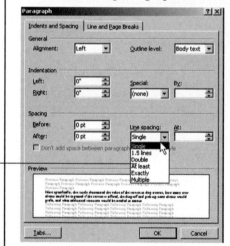

4. Choose OK.

   Or: On the keyboard, press:
   - CTRL+1 for single spacing
   - CTRL+5 for 1.5 spacing
   - CTRL+2 for double spacing

(continued on next page)

Or: On the formatting toolbar, click the drop down arrow on the Line Spacing button. Select the desired line spacing option.

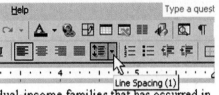

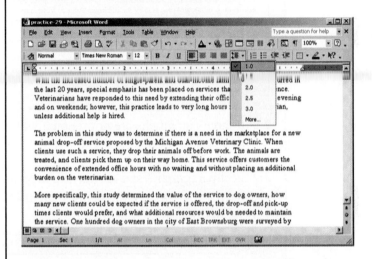

Note: If you change line spacing at the beginning of a document, all paragraphs that you type will reflect the new spacing unless you change the spacing again. If you change the line spacing in an existing paragraph, only the lines of that paragraph are changed.

(continued on next page)

PRACTICE

1. Open the file named *practice-29*.

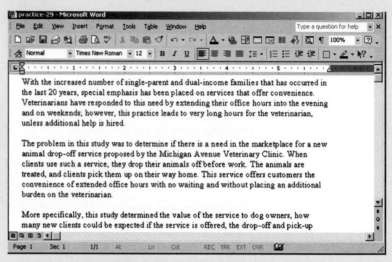

Reminder: To select a paragraph, triple-click anywhere in the paragraph.

2. All three paragraphs are now shown with single-spaced lines. Select paragraph 2 and change the line spacing to 1.5, using the keyboard shortcut (CTRL+5).

3. Select paragraph 3 and change the lines to double spacing.

4. Save the file with the file name *student-29*.

5. Print the file.

Your printout should look similar to this:

Single spacing

1.5 spacing

Double spacing

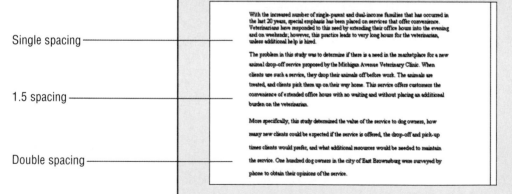

6. Close the file named *student-29*.

7. Return to GDP.

Go To
Textbook

Lesson 30

Academic Reports with Displays

Increase Indent

Numbers and bulleted lists should be indented to the same point as the indented paragraphs in a document. To position a list at the same point as an indented paragraph, use the Increase Indent button on the Formatting toolbar.

To position a list at the same position as an indented paragraph:

1. Create the bulleted or numbered list.
2. Select the list.
3. On the Formatting toolbar, click the Increase Indent button as many times as needed to position the bullets or numbers at the same point as an indented paragraph.

Note: If you indent the list too much, click the Decrease Indent button as needed.

Increase
Indent button

DOUBLE INDENT

Paragraphs can be indented from both the left and right margins (double indent) to set off a quoted paragraph having 4 lines or more or a paragraph that needs special emphasis.

To format a displayed paragraph with a double indent:

1. Type the displayed paragraph and the paragraph immediately following it.
2. Select only the lines to be included in the displayed paragraph and change the line spacing to single.
3. On the menu, choose Format, **P**aragraph.
4. If necessary, click the **I**ndents and Spacing tab.

(continued on next page)

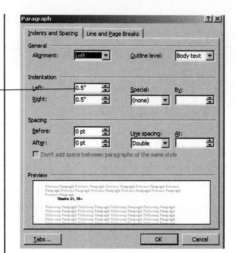

Type how much you want the text indented from each margin.

5. In the Indentation box, type the amount of space you want the text indented from the left and right margin (typically, 0.5 inch from each margin).

6. Choose OK.

7. Click immediately after the last period in the displayed paragraph, and press ENTER 1 time to insert 1 blank line after the displayed paragraph.

PRACTICE

1. Open the file named *practice-30*.

2. Select the second paragraph ("How can you . . . ") and change the line spacing to single.

3. Format the paragraph with a 0.5-inch double indent.

4. Insert 1 blank line after the paragraph.

(continued on next page)

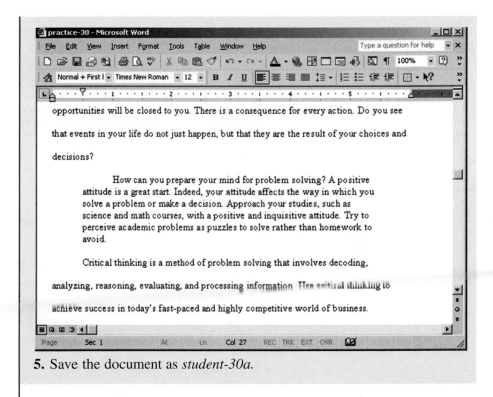

opportunities will be closed to you. There is a consequence for every action. Do you see

that events in your life do not just happen, but that they are the result of your choices and

decisions?

How can you prepare your mind for problem solving? A positive attitude is a great start. Indeed, your attitude affects the way in which you solve a problem or make a decision. Approach your studies, such as science and math courses, with a positive and inquisitive attitude. Try to perceive academic problems as puzzles to solve rather than homework to avoid.

Critical thinking is a method of problem solving that involves decoding,

analyzing, reasoning, evaluating, and processing information. Use critical thinking to

achieve success in today's fast-paced and highly competitive world of business.

5. Save the document as *student-30a*.

Cut, Copy, and Paste

You can move or copy text from one part of a document to another. To *move* text means to first cut (delete) the selected text from one location and then paste (insert) it in another location (either in the same document or in a different document). To *copy* text means to make a copy of the selected text and then insert (paste) it in another location; copying leaves the original text unchanged.

To cut and paste (move) text:

1. Select the text you want to move.

Cut   Copy   Paste
button   button   button

(continued on next page)

The sentence to be moved is selected (highlighted).

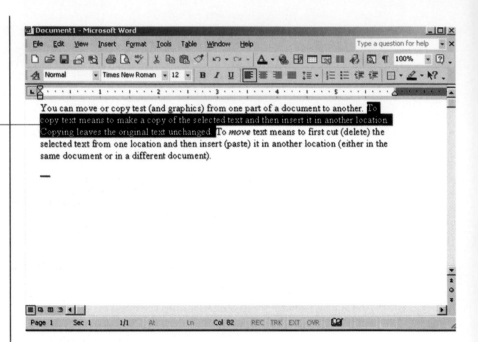

2. On the toolbar, click the Cut button.

Or: On the menu, choose **E**dit, Cu**t**.

Or: On the keyboard, press CTRL+X.

The Office Clipboard contains separate clipboards. It is used to collect items without erasing previous items. To display the Office Clipboard, choose **E**dit from the menu bar, Office Clipboard. The Office Clip**b**oard Task Pane window opens on the right hand side of the document. The text stored in the clipboard can be pasted as often as needed.

Note: The Paste Options button appears on the document when you paste. Press ESC to close the Paste Options button.

(continued on next page)

The selected sentence has been moved from the document to the clipboard, a temporary storage area.

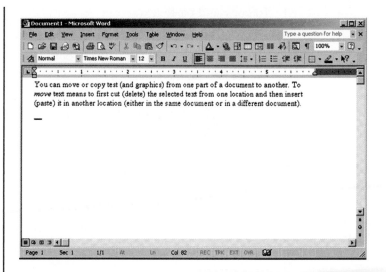

3. Position the insertion point where you want to insert the text.

4. On the toolbar, click the Paste button.

    Or: On the menu, choose **E**dit, **P**aste.

    Or: On the keyboard, press CTRL+V.

    The selected text reappears in its new location.

The selected sentence has been— pasted from the clipboard into its new location.

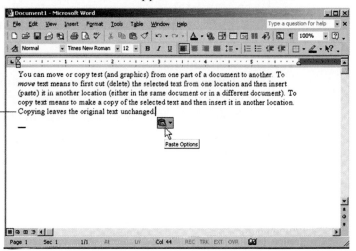

Hint: Always check the revised text to ensure that you moved exactly what you wanted to move and that the spacing and punctuation are correct.

(continued on next page)

To copy and paste text:

1. Select the text you want to copy.
2. On the toolbar, click the Copy button.

   Or: On the menu, choose **E**dit, **C**opy.

   Or: On the keyboard, press CTRL+C.

   The original text remains in place, but a copy of it has been placed on the clipboard.
3. Position the insertion point where you want to insert the copied text.
4. On the toolbar, click the Paste button.

   Or: On the menu, choose **E**dit, **P**aste.

   Or: On the keyboard, press CTRL+V.

   The selected text reappears in its new location.

The keyboard shortcuts for Cut (CTRL+X), Copy (CTRL+C), and Paste (CTRL+V) can be used in any Windows program—for example, database or spreadsheet programs.

Note: Word also allows moving or copying by using "Drag and Drop Editing." To learn how to drag and drop, click the Microsoft Word Help button and type *drag and drop*. Click **S**earch.

PRACTICE

1. Open the file named *practice-30a*.
2. Transpose the two numbered paragraphs at the end of the document:
   a. Select the second numbered paragraph and be sure to include the paragraph symbol at the end of the paragraph. ("Try to perceive . . ."). Note that you cannot select the paragraph number because it was created using the Numbering command.
   b. Cut the paragraph.
   c. Position the insertion point to the left of the "A" in "A positive . . ."
   d. Paste the cut paragraph in this location. Note that the paragraphs have been automatically renumbered.

   Your screen should now look like the following:

(continued on next page)

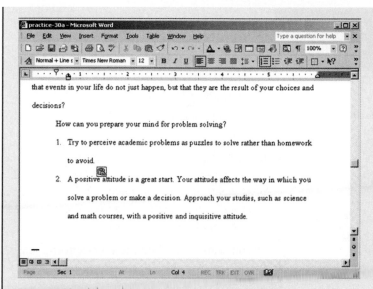

that events in your life do not just happen, but that they are the result of your choices and

decisions?

How can you prepare your mind for problem solving?

1. Try to perceive academic problems as puzzles to solve rather than homework
   to avoid.

2. A positive attitude is a great start. Your attitude affects the way in which you
   solve a problem or make a decision. Approach your studies, such as science
   and math courses, with a positive and inquisitive attitude.

3. Save the file with the file name *student-30b*.

4. Return to GDP.

Business Letters

Insert Date

Date Insert (text) is the default setting.

You can have Word insert the correct date into your document as either text or as a field. When you insert the date as text, the current date is inserted, and it never changes. Thus, if you open the same document next week, it will still have the date you created the document rather than the current date. (This is exactly what you want for most business documents.)

If you want to update the date automatically each time you print a document (for example, in a form letter), you would insert the date as a field.

To insert the date into a document:

1. Position the insertion point where you want the date to appear.
2. Choose **I**nsert, Date and **T**ime.
3. Select the date format.

This is the typical format for most business documents.

Date and Time	? ×
Available formats:	**L**anguage:
12/28/2001 Friday, December 28, 2001 December 28, 2001 12/28/01 2001-12-28 28-Dec-01 12.28.2001 Dec. 28, 01 28 December 2001 December 01 Dec-01 12/28/2001 11:47 AM 12/28/2001 11:47:25 AM 11:47 AM 11:47:25 AM 11:47 11:47:25	English (U.S.)
	☐ **U**pdate automatically
Default...	OK Cancel

Select this box only if you want to update the date automatically whenever you open the document.

4. Choose OK.
   Or: On the keyboard, press ALT+SHIFT+D.
   Note: If you insert the date using the shortcut keys, the date will be entered in MM/DD/YY format (for example, 11/11/02) unless you changed the format in the Date and Time dialog box.

(continued on next page)

Go To

Textbook

PRACTICE

1. Open the file named *practice-31*.
2. Place the insertion point at the beginning of the letter and press ENTER 6 times to position the date 2 inches from the top margin.
3. Delete the existing date and use the Insert Date command to insert the current date as text.
4. Save the file with the file name *student-31*.
5. Return to GDP.

Note: If the date contains a dotted rcd underline with a Smart Tag actions button, press ESC to clear the button.

Lesson 33 — Envelopes

Envelopes

Word makes it easy to format and print envelopes. In fact, if you type a letter first, Word can almost always identify the inside address and automatically insert it into the envelope window so that you don't have to retype it.

To format an envelope:

1. On the menu, choose **T**ools, **Le**tters and Mailings, **E**nvelopes and Labels.

2. Select the **E**nvelopes tab if it is not already active.

Word searches your document for what "looks like" an inside address and inserts it into the **D**elivery address window.

A No. 10 envelope is the default setting. Choose **O**ptions to select another envelope size.

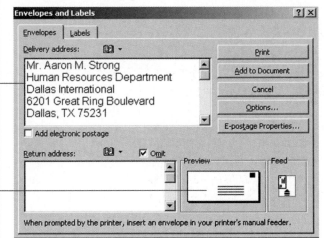

3. If you have not created a letter, type the delivery address. If you have a letter displayed on screen, check the delivery address and edit it as necessary.

4. Type a return address; or if you are using an envelope with a printed return address, be sure the **R**eturn Address box is empty or click the O**m**it check box.

5. Insert an envelope in the correct position into your printer and choose **P**rint.

Note: If you want to save the envelope, choose **A**dd to Document. Word adds (appends) the envelope to a blank document if you have not created a letter, or to the letter if you have one displayed on screen. Any time you print the letter, you will also print the envelope. You may need to make special adjustments to your printer in order to print an envelope.

(continued on next page)

PRACTICE

1. Open the file named *practice-31.*

2. Choose the Letters and Mailings, **E**nvelopes and Labels command from the **T**ools menu.

Your screen should look like this:

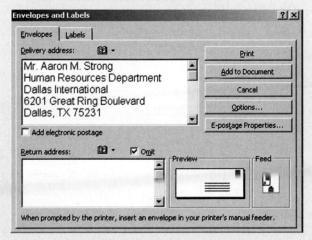

3. Insert a No. 10 envelope into the printer and print the envelope.

Your printed envelope should look like this:

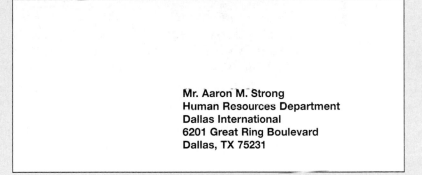

Mr. Aaron M. Strong
Human Resources Department
Dallas International
6201 Great Ring Boulevard
Dallas, TX 75231

4. Close the document. When prompted to save changes, choose **N**o.

(continued on next page)

Labels

It is easy to print labels to be used as a return address or a delivery address. You can print a full page of the same label or a single label. You can also choose from a variety of label sizes.

To print a single label:

1. Open a new file.
2. From the menu, choose **T**ools, L**e**tters and Mailings, **E**nvelopes and Labels.
3. Click the **L**abels tab.

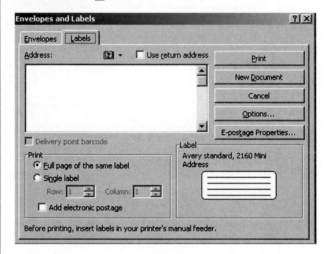

4. Type the mailing address in the **A**ddress box.

Note: If you open the Envelopes and Labels dialog box with an active document, Word will search for an address and insert it automatically.

5. Clear the check box for Use **r**eturn address, if necessary.
6. Click Si**ng**le label.
7. Click the **O**ptions button.

(continued on next page)

Choose the label format for the labels you will be using.

Note the details under Label information.

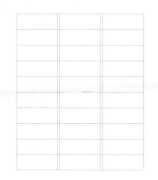

This is the blank label form for Avery 5160 address labels.

Label Options   ? X

Printer information
- ○ Dot matrix
- ● Laser and ink jet   Tray: Manual Paper Feed ▼

Label information

Label products: Avery standard ▼

Product number:

5096 – Diskette	Label information	
5097 – Diskette	Type:	Address
5159 – Address	Height:	1"
5160 – Address	Width:	2.63"
5161 – Address	Page size:	Letter (8 ½ x 11 in)
5162 – Address		
5163 – Shipping		

[Details...] [New Label...] [Delete] [OK] [Cancel]

8. Choose 5160 – Address from the Product number list.
9. Click OK.
10. Click Print.

To print a full page of the same label:

1. Open a new file.
2. From the menu, choose **T**ools, **E**nvelopes and Labels.
3. Click the **L**abels tab.
4. Type the mailing address in the **A**ddress box.
5. Clear the check box for Use **r**eturn address, if necessary.
6. Click **F**ull page of the same label.
7. Click the **O**ptions button.
8. Choose 5160 – Address from the Product number list and click OK.
9. Click New **D**ocument.
10. Print the document.
11. Close the document. When prompted to save changes, choose **N**o.

PRACTICE

1. Open a new file.
2. Open the Envelopes and Labels dialog box.
3. Click the **L**abels tab.
4. Delete any text that might appear in the **A**ddress box.
5. Clear the check box for Use **r**eturn address, if necessary.
6. Click **F**ull page of the same label.
7. Click the **O**ptions button.
8. Choose 5160 – Address from the Product number list.
9. Click OK.

(continued on next page)

10. Click New **D**ocument. A full page of empty labels appears.
11. Type the following information in the first label.

```
<Student Name>
Stevenson Corporation
1479 Monroe Street
Gastonia, NC 28054
```

12. Press TAB twice or click in the next label (middle label in first row) and type the following information.

```
Mr. George Shawley
1014 South Marietta Street
Grove City, PA 16127
```

13. Print the document.
14. Close the document. When prompted to save changes, choose **N**o.
15. Return to GDP.

Go To
Textbook

Correspondence Review

Italic and Underline

One way to emphasize text (such as book or magazine titles) is to format the text in italic or underline.

To italicize or underline text as you type:

_I_   **_U_**

Italic button   Underline button

1. On the toolbar, click the Italic or Underline button.
   Or: On the keyboard, press CTRL+I (italic) or CTRL+U (underline).
2. Type the text you want to appear in italic or underline.
3. Choose the Italic or Underline command again to turn off italic or underline.
   The text appears on screen in italic or underline.

plain text

italic text

<u>underlined text</u>

To italicize or underline existing text:

1. Select the text to be italicized or underlined.
2. Click the Italic or Underline button or press CTRL+I or CTRL+U.

Reminder: Another way to emphasize text is to format it in bold.

Note: Italic and Underline are toggle commands. Choosing the command once turns the feature on; choosing the command twice in succession turns the feature on and then off. If you italicize or underline text by accident, select the text and then choose the command again.

PRACTICE

1. Open a blank document.
2. Type the following paragraph exactly as it appears (but let word wrap end your lines for you):

   I will <u>not</u> have time to read *To Kill a Mockingbird* before Friday. I will have time to read This Old House.

3. In the second sentence, underline the word "will" and italicize the title "This Old House."
4. In the first sentence, delete the underline from the word "not."

(continued on next page)

Your screen should now look like this:

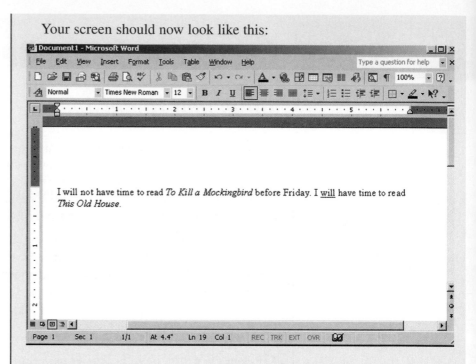

I will not have time to read *To Kill a Mockingbird* before Friday. I <u>will</u> have time to read *This Old House*.

5. Save the file with the file name *student-35*.

6. Return to GDP.

Boxed Tables

Table—Create

A table consists of *columns* and *rows* displayed on screen with borders. Columns run from top to bottom and rows run from left to right. A cell is the intersection of a row and a column. When you type text in a cell, the text can wrap to the next line of the cell, just as in a regular document. The cell expands vertically to make room for the next line.

The vertical columns are labeled by letters and the horizontal rows are labeled by numbers. Thus, the practice table below has two columns (labeled A and B) and five rows (labeled 1 through 5). The first item of text in the last line of the table ("Faculty Sponsor") is in Cell A5.

	A	B
1	President	Juanita Cortes-Perin
2	Vice President	Paul J. Anchor
3	Secretary	Rhetta Jones
4	Treasurer	Imogene Corker
5	Faculty Sponsor	Professor Leon South

PRACTICE

Insert Table button

To create a table:

1. Position the insertion point where you want the table to start (in our case, at the top of the document).
2. On the Standard toolbar, click the Insert Table button; then drag to create a table with five rows and two columns (a 5 × 2 table).

   Or: On the menu, choose T**a**ble, **I**nsert, **T**able.

   The Insert Table dialog box appears.

(continued on next page)

- Enter the number of columns you want in the Number of **c**olumns box; for our practice table, type 2.

- Press TAB and enter the number of rows in the Number of **r**ows box; in this case, type 5.

- Choose OK.

The table outline is inserted into your document. To move from cell to cell, click the cell with the mouse or press TAB. To move to the previous cell, press SHIFT+TAB. Use the arrow keys to move up or down the rows.

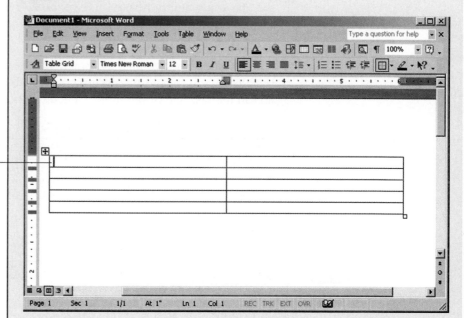

The table outline, with the insertion point in Cell A1.

If you press ENTER by accident, an additional blank line will be added to the cell. Press BACKSPACE or click UNDO to delete the unwanted line.

If you are in the last cell of a table (Cell B5 in this case), pressing TAB would insert an additional row into the table. Click the Undo button to cancel the unwanted command.

3. If necessary, place the insertion point in Cell A1 (the first cell) and then begin typing the table information. For this table, type `President`.

4. Press TAB to move to Cell B1 and type `Juanita Cortes-Perin`.

5. Press TAB (*not* ENTER) to move to Cell A2 and continue typing the table. Here is our practice table:

```
President              Juanita Cortes-Perin
Vice President         Paul J. Anchor
Secretary              Rhetta Jones
Treasurer              Imogene Corker
Faculty Sponsor        Professor Leon South
```

(continued on next page)

Your finished table should look like this:

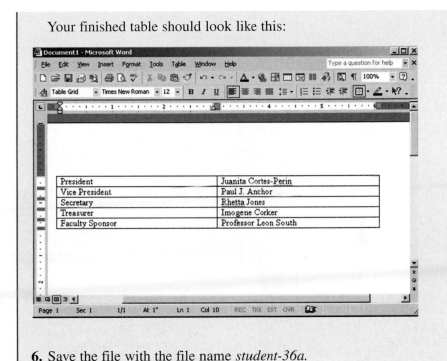

President	Juanita Cortes-Perin
Vice President	Paul J. Anchor
Secretary	Rhetta Jones
Treasurer	Imogene Corker
Faculty Sponsor	Professor Leon South

6. Save the file with the file name *student-36a*.

Table—AutoFit to Contents

To resize the width of columns in a table to fit the contents in that table, apply the AutoFit to Contents feature.

1. Position the insertion point in the table.

2. From the menu, choose Table, AutoFit, AutoFit to Contents.

The **A**utoFit option automatically resizes the table without changing any other formatting.

(continued on next page)

3. The table has been resized to accommodate the longest word or words in each column.

PRACTICE

1. If necessary, open the file named *student-36a*.

2. Place the insertion point in the table.

3. Choose **A**utoFit from the **Ta**ble menu and Auto**F**it to Contents.

4. Your finished table should look like this:

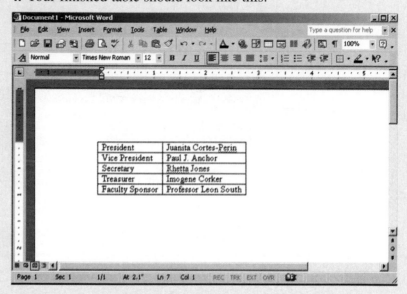

5. Save the file with the file name *student-36b*.

6. Return to GDP.

Open Tables with Titles

Table—Merge Cells

Table titles (and subtitles, if used) are typed in the first row of a table. In order to have the title centered over all columns of the table, you must merge the cells in that row to form one cell that extends the entire width of the table.

To merge cells:

1. Select the cells you want to merge.

President	Juanita Cortes-Perin
Vice President	Paul J. Anchor
Secretary	Rhetta Jones
Treasurer	Imogene Corker
Faculty Sponsor	Professor Leon South

Merge Cells button

2. From the menu, choose T**a**ble, **M**erge Cells, or click the Merge Cells button on the Tables and Borders toolbar (if displayed).
The selected cells are merged into a single cell.

President	Juanita Cortes-Perin
Vice President	Paul J. Anchor
Secretary	Rhetta Jones
Treasurer	Imogene Corker
Faculty Sponsor	Professor Leon South

You can use your usual formats (such as center and bold) when creating a table.

3. Type the information you want in the merged cell.

PHI MU ALPHA CHAPTER OFFICERS	
President	Juanita Cortes-Perin
Vice President	Paul J. Anchor
Secretary	Rhetta Jones
Treasurer	Imogene Corker
Faculty Sponsor	Professor Leon South

Note: Standard format is to center and type a table title in bold and all caps and to insert 1 blank line after the title. Type a subtitle, if used, below the title using upper and lowercase and bold formatting.

(continued on next page)

Note: It doesn't matter whether you first merge the cells and then type the title or whether you first type the title and then merge the cells. The result is the same.

PRACTICE

1. Open the file named *practice-37*.

Row 1

Site Visitation	September 13-16	Alan C. Wingett
On-Site Interviews	September 14-15	Chad Spencer
Preliminary Decisions	September 23	Sherri Jordan
New York Visits	October 4-7	Pedro Martin
Evaluation Conference	October 8	Sherri Jordan
Final Decision	October 10	Gerald J. Pearson

2. Select Row 1.

3. On the menu choose T**a**ble, **M**erge Cells, or click Merge Cells on the Tables and Borders toolbar.

4. Turn on bold and center alignment, and type the title in all caps: **VICE PRESIDENTIAL SEARCH SCHEDULE.**

5. Turn off bold, press ENTER, and type the subtitle Harry Wesson, Coordinator.

6. Press ENTER 1 time to insert a blank line after the subtitle.

Your table should look like this:

VICE PRESIDENTIAL SEARCH SCHEDULE Harry Wesson, Coordinator		
Site Visitation	September 13-16	Alan C. Wingett
On-Site Interviews	September 14-15	Chad Spencer
Preliminary Decisions	September 23	Sherri Jordan
New York Visits	October 4-7	Pedro Martin
Evaluation Conference	October 8	Sherri Jordan
Final Decision	October 10	Gerald J. Pearson

7. Save your file with the file name *student-37*.

(continued on next page)

Table—Borders

The lines surrounding each cell in a table can be changed. You can format the left, right, top, bottom, and inside lines bordering a cell differently. You can also remove lines around each cell in a table (that is, to switch from a *boxed* to an *open* format):

1. Position the insertion point anywhere in the table.
2. On the menu, choose Format, **B**orders and Shading; then click the **B**orders tab.
3. In the Setting section, select **N**one.
4. Choose OK. The table now has no lines.

Note: The table will appear on screen with gridlines. These will not appear on the printed copy.

To add, change, or delete borders on any side of a cell.

1. Position the insertion point in the cell to which you want to apply borders.
2. From the menu, choose Format, **B**orders and Shading. Select the **B**orders tab if it is not already active.
3. In the Borders and Shading dialog box, in the St**y**le box, choose the line style.
4. In the **W**idth box, click the down arrow, then choose the line width.

Select **W**idth————

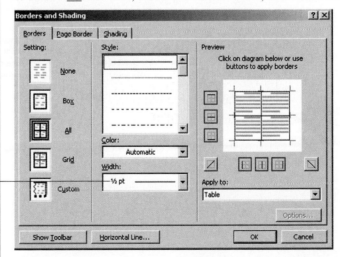

5. In the Preview box, click either the sides of the diagram or the appropriate buttons to position the borders where you want them: top, bottom, left, right, or inside. Click OK. To create ruled tables, click the top and bottom border buttons. Click OK.

(continued on next page)

Outside Border button

Note: Clicking the Outside Border button on the Formatting toolbar will create a border with the line style previously selected. Clicking the down arrow to the right of the Outside Border button on the Formatting toolbar will enable you to position the borders at the top, bottom, left, right, or inside.

PRACTICE

1. If necessary, open the file named *student-37* and verify that the insertion point is in the first cell.
2. On the menu, choose F**o**rmat, **B**orders and Shading.
3. Click the **B**orders tab.
4. Select the **N**one option.
5. Choose OK. Choose Print Preview.
6. Close Print Preview.
7. Select the first row of the table and open the Borders and Shading dialog box.
8. Change the width to 3 pt and click the bottom border button.
9. Click OK.

   Your finished table should look like this.

VICE PRESIDENTIAL SEARCH SCHEDULE Harry Wesson, Coordinator		
Site Visitation	September 13-16	Alan C. Wingett
On-Site Interviews	September 14-15	Chad Spencer
Preliminary Decisions	September 23	Sherri Jordan
New York Visits	October 4-7	Pedro Martin
Evaluation Conference	October 8	Sherri Jordan
Final Decision	October 10	Gerald J. Pearson

10. Save the file with the file name *student-37b*.
11. Return to GDP.

Go To
Textbook

Open Tables with Column Headings

Center a Table Horizontally

When you create a table, the table extends from margin to margin by default. However, if you adjust column widths, the table becomes left-aligned.

To change the horizontal alignment of a table:

1. Position the insertion point in the table.

2. From the menu, choose T**a**ble, Table P**r**operties.

3. Select the **T**able tab, if necessary.

Select **C**enter to center a table horizontally.

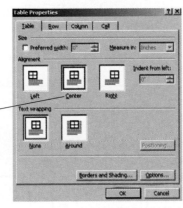

4. Select the alignment option desired (in this case, **C**enter).

5. Choose OK.

(continued on next page)

If you choose **C**enter, the table is centered between the margins, as shown below:

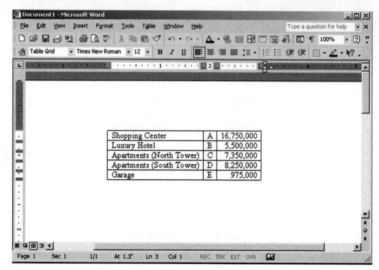

6. From the menu, choose **V**iew, **P**rint Layout to see the document centered.

PRACTICE

1. Open the file named *practice-38*.
2. From the menu, choose T**a**ble, **A**utoFit, AutoFit to Contents.
   Your table should now look like this:

Vehicle	1999	2000	2001
Sedan	17,861	18,216	20,743
SUV	25,700	26,562	29,270
Truck	15,600	17,247	18,983

3. Select Row 2 (the column headings) and bold and center them.
4. Select Row 1 (the blank row) and merge the cells (from the menu, choose T**a**ble, **M**erge Cells).
5. Center and type the table title PRICE COMPARISONS in bold in Row 1; then press ENTER to leave 1 blank line after the title.

(continued on next page)

6. Center the table horizontally. From the menu, choose T**a**ble, Table **P**roperties. Select the **T**able tab if necessary, and choose **C**enter in the Alignment section; then choose OK.

Your finished table should now look like this:

PRICE COMPARISONS			
Vehicle	1999	2000	2001
Sedan	17,861	18,216	20,743
SUV	25,700	26,562	29,270
Truck	15,600	17,247	18,983

7. Save the file with the file name *student-38a*.

Center Page

Use the Page Setup command to center text vertically on a page (see the illustration below).

Before vertical centering, the table is too high on the page.

After vertical centering, the table looks balanced on the page.

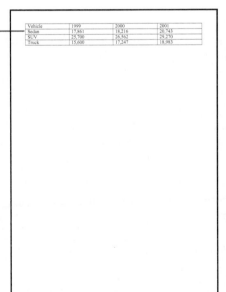

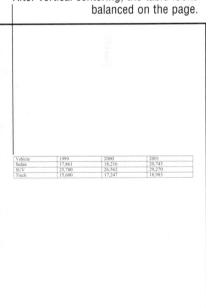

To center text (such as a table) vertically on a page:

1. Position the insertion point anywhere on the page you want centered.

2. On the menu, choose **F**ile, Page Set**u**p.

(continued on next page)

3. Select the **L**ayout tab.

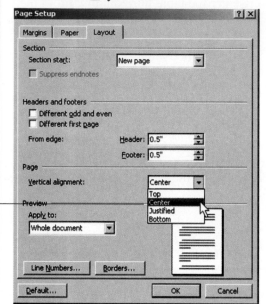

The center option creates equal top and bottom margins.

4. Click the down arrow in the **V**ertical alignment list box, and select Center.

5. Choose OK.

Note: In Normal View, Word does not show the document as centered on your screen.

PRACTICE

1. If necessary, open the file named *student-38a*.
2. Center the table vertically on the page.
3. Choose Print Preview to view the centered table.
4. Save the file with the file name *student-38b*.
5. Return to GDP.

Ruled Tables with Number Columns

Table—Align Text in a Column

You can improve the readability and appearance of a table by changing the column alignment.

To align text in columns:

1. Select the cells to format.

2. Use the Formatting toolbar, the Format menu or the keyboard to select Left, Center, Right, or Justified alignment.

Keyboard shortcut reminder:
Left = CTRL+L
Center = CTRL+E
Right = CTRL+R
Justified = CTRL+J

Tables and Borders toolbar

PRACTICE

1. Open the file named *practice-39*.

Section	Type	Capacity
A	Orchestra	350
B	Main	1,200
C	Balcony	460
D	Handicapped	32

(continued on next page)

2. Select the four data cells in column A (items A-D) and center them (CTRL+E).

3. Select the four data cells in column C (the capacity figures) and right-align them (CTRL+R).

4. Click inside the table and apply the Auto**F**it to Contents feature.

5. Select row 2 (the column headings) and bold them.

6. Left-align the headings for column A and column B. Right-align the heading for column C.

7. Select row 1 (the blank row) and merge the cells.

8. Center and type the table title AVALON SEATING CAPACITY in bold in row 1; then press ENTER to leave 1 blank line after the title.

9. Click inside the table. Choose F**o**rmat, **B**orders and shading from the Menu bar. Choose the **B**orders tab. In the Setting box, choose None. Click OK.

10. Select the heading row of the table (Selection, Type and Capacity). Choose F**o**rmat, **B**orders and Shading, **B**orders tab. In the Preview box at the right, click the top and bottom border buttons. Click OK.

11. Select the last row of the table. Choose F**o**rmat, **B**orders and Shading, select the **B**orders tab. From the Preview Box, click the bottom border button. Click OK.

Your finished table should now look like this:

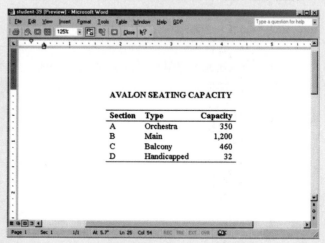

12. Save the file with the file name *student-39*.

13. Return to GDP.

Go To
Textbook

Lesson 41

Business Reports with Footnotes

Footnotes

Typing footnotes with Word is easy because the program automatically numbers, positions, and formats the footnotes for you. All you have to do is give the Footnote command.

To insert a footnote:

1. Position the insertion point in the text where you want the footnote reference to appear (do *not* type the footnote number).

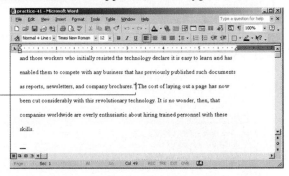

Position the insertion point where you want the footnote to appear.

2. Change to Normal View.

3. On the menu, choose **I**nsert, Refere**n**ce, Foot**n**ote.

The Footnote and Endnote dialog box appears:

(continued on next page)

4. Choose **I**nsert to accept the default settings.

Or: Instead of Steps 2–3, on the keyboard, press ALT+CTRL+F.

The screen splits to show a note pane at the bottom (you must be in Normal View) and the footnote number appears.

Footnote numbers are automatically inserted.

Note pane

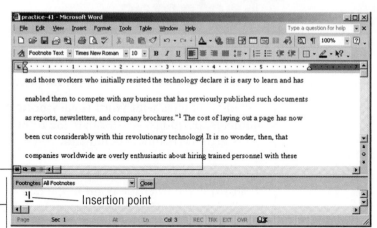

Insertion point

The default format for footnotes in Word is to number them with Arabic numerals and begin them at the left margin.

5. Type the footnote reference. Do *not* press ENTER after typing the footnote.

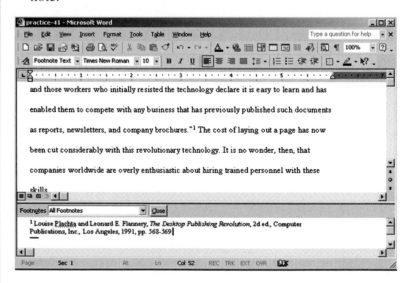

(continued on next page)

6. Click **C**lose to return to your document screen.

Word inserts a divider line and automatically keeps track of numbering footnotes as you add or delete notes in a report. To view the footnotes on the screen, you must change from Normal to Print Layout View.

Regardless of which view you're in, the report page with footnotes will print correctly, as illustrated below.

Word formats footnotes in a smaller font size than normal text.

> and those workers who initially resisted the technology declare it is easy to learn and has
>
> enabled them to compete with any business that has previously published such documents
>
> as reports, newsletters, and company brochures."[1] The cost of laying out a page has now
>
> been cut considerably with this revolutionary technology.[2] It is no wonder, then, that
>
> companies worldwide are overly enthusiastic about hiring trained personnel with these
>
> skills.
>
> _____
>
> [1] Louise Plachta and Leonard E. Flannery, *The Desktop Publishing Revolution*, 2d ed., Computer Publications, Inc., Los Angeles, 1991, pp. 558-559.
> [2] Terry Denton, "Newspaper Cuts Costs, Increases Quality," The Monthly Press, October 1992, p. 160.

To edit a footnote:

1. Double-click the footnote number in the document window.
2. Make whatever changes are needed.

To delete a footnote:

1. Select the footnote number in the document.
2. Press DELETE.

PRACTICE

1. Open the file named *practice-41*.
2. Position the insertion point immediately after the ending quotation mark in the first sentence and insert the footnote shown below:
   Reminder: Do not type the footnote number; Word does it for you.

   [1]Louise Plachta and Leonard E. Flannery, *The Desktop Publishing Revolution*, 2d ed., Computer Publications, Inc., Los Angeles, 1991, pp. 568-569.

3. Position the insertion point immediately after the period in the second sentence and insert the following footnote:

   [2]Terry Denton, "Newspaper Cuts Costs, Increases Quality," *The Monthly Press*, October 1992, p. 160.

(continued on next page)

4. Edit Footnote 1 by changing the page references to pp. 558–559.

5. Print your document; it should look similar to the following report page:

2

and those workers who initially resisted the technology declare it is easy to learn and has

enabled them to compete with any business that has previously published such documents

as reports, newsletters, and company brochures."[1] The cost of laying out a page has now

been cut considerably with this revolutionary technology.[2] It is no wonder, then, that

companies worldwide are overly enthusiastic about hiring trained personnel with these

skills.

_____

[1] Louise Plachta and Leonard E. Flannery, *The Desktop Publishing Revolution*, 2d ed., Computer
Publications, Inc., Los Angeles, 1991, pp. 558-559.
[2] Terry Denton, "Newspaper Cuts Costs, Increases Quality," *The Monthly Press*, October 1992, p. 160.

Note that the footnote references are positioned at the bottom of a page—even on an incomplete page.

Go To
Textbook

6. Save the file with the file name *student-41*.

7. Return to GDP.

Academic Reports in APA Style

Margins

Margins represent the distance between the edge of the paper and the text. Word default margins are 1.25-inch left and right margins and 1-inch top and bottom margins. If you change margin settings, the changes affect the entire document—not just the current page.

To change margins:

1. Position the insertion point at the beginning of the document.

2. On the menu, choose **F**ile, Page Set**u**p.

The Page Setup dialog box appears.

Note: If the **M**argins tab is not active, select the **M**argins tab.

Type in the new margins.

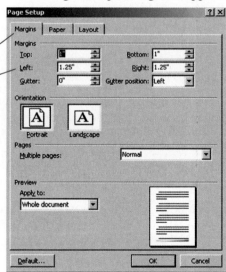

3. Select the **M**argins tab if it is not already active.

4. Type the new margin settings or click the arrows to increase or decrease the margins you want to change.

5. Click OK.

(continued on next page)

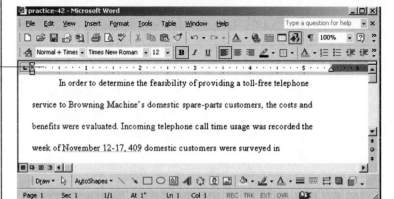

The ruler indicates a 6-inch line of writing (the default setting for 1.25-inch side margins).

The ruler now indicates a 5.5-inch line of writing (the setting after switching to 1.5-inch side margins).

Print Layout View will display the top margin on the vertical ruler.

Word is preset to display the ruler. However, if the ruler is not visible, you should know how to redisplay it.

To display (or hide) the ruler:

On the menu, choose **V**iew, **R**uler. The menu command will have a check mark beside it when the ruler is displayed.

Note: For a bound report you would change only the left margin. To increase the left margin 0.5 inch, set the left margin at 1.75 inches.

Hands
On

PRACTICE

1. Open the file named *practice-42*.
2. Print the file.
3. Change the top margin to 2 inches.
4. Change the left and right margins to 1.5 inches.
5. Print the first page of the revised document and compare it with the original printout.

(continued on next page)

6. Save the file with the name *student-42a*.

In order to determine the feasibility of providing a toll-free telephone service to Browning Machine's domestic spare-parts customers, the costs and benefits were evaluated. Incoming telephone call time usage was recorded the week of November 12-17, 409 domestic customers were surveyed in October/November, and a telephone interview was conducted with an AT&T toll-free representative in October. The criteria used were the costs and benefits of a toll-free service, the value customers place on a toll-free service, and how to communicate a toll-free service.

Browning Machine currently uses AT&T as their long-distance telephone carrier. The required toll-free telephone service and cost analysis are based on information from, and a telephone interview with AT&T.

According to Art Neumann, an AT&T Long-Distance Network Sales Specialist, the service recommended for Browning Machine is AT&T Readyline. Readyline is an inward toll-free service that utilizes the existing telephone lines to receive the 800-number calls.

The advantage of this service is all of the existing lines currently used to place and receive calls are available to receive the incoming 800-number calls. Because the Readyline service distributes the incoming calls among the available lines, there is a reduction in the chance a caller will receive a busy signal. Several customers indicated in the comment section of the questionnaire that if Browning were to offer an 800 number, they should include sufficient service to handle the expected volume of incoming calls.

In order to determine the feasibility of providing a toll-free telephone service to Browning Machine's domestic spare-parts customers, the costs and benefits were evaluated. Incoming telephone call time usage was recorded the week of November 12-17, 409 domestic customers were surveyed in October/November, and a telephone interview was conducted with an AT&T toll-free representative in October. The criteria used were the costs and benefits of a toll-free service, the value customers place on a toll-free service, and how to communicate a toll-free service.

Browning Machine currently uses AT&T as their long-distance telephone carrier. The required toll-free telephone service and cost analysis are based on information from, and a telephone interview with AT&T.

According to Art Neumann, an AT&T Long-Distance Network Sales Specialist, the service recommended for Browning Machine is AT&T Readyline. Readyline is an inward toll-free service that utilizes the existing telephone lines to receive the 800-number calls.

The advantage of this service is all of the existing lines currently used to place and receive calls are available to receive the incoming 800-number calls. Because the Readyline service distributes the incoming calls among lines, there is a reduction in the chance a caller will receive a busy signal. Several

Original page 1   Revised page 1

7. Close the file.

Headers and Footers

A *header* is text that is positioned inside the top margin and can be printed on every page in a document. A *footer* is text that is positioned inside the bottom margin. The header or footer can be as simple as the page number or as complex as text plus lines and graphics.

To add a header or footer to a document:

1. Position the insertion point at the beginning of the document (or on the first page where the header or footer is to appear).

2. On the menu, choose **V**iew, **H**eader and Footer. The regular document text is dimmed and the Header and Footer toolbar is displayed.

(continued on next page)

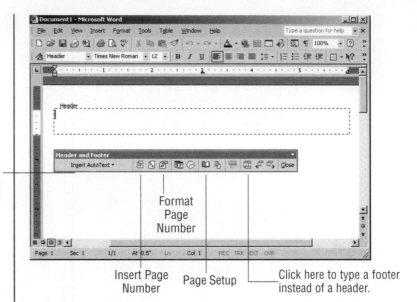

The Header and Footer toolbar displays the buttons you will need to format headers and footers.

Format Page Number

Insert Page Number

Page Setup

Click here to type a footer instead of a header.

Switch Between Header and Footer button

To delete a header or footer, select the text and press Delete.

3. Type the text for the header or footer, using regular editing and formatting techniques. (Click the Switch Between Header and Footer button on the Header and Footer toolbar to switch to the footer.) If you have a multiline header, press ENTER once after the last line to leave a blank line between the header and the document text.

Note: To insert the current date or page number, click the appropriate button. To start the page numbering at a different page, click the Format Page Number button. In the Page number Format dialog box, choose Start **a**t, then type the desired page number.

Note: The date format will be determined by the format previously selected. It may be necessary to choose the Date command from the Insert menu to select the date format preferred.

4. Choose the **C**lose button on the toolbar to return to the document.

Normally, Word displays the same header and footer on all pages. Sometimes, however, you may not want a header or footer to appear on the first page.

To delete the header and footer from the first page:

1. On the menu, choose **V**iew, **H**eader and Footer.
2. Click the Page Setup button on the Header and Footer toolbar.
3. Select the **L**ayout tab to display the page layout options.

Page Setup button

(continued on next page)

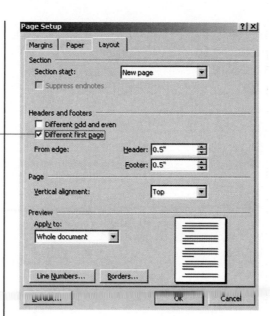

Select the Different first **p**age check box.

4. Under Headers and Footers, select the Different first **p**age check box.

5. Choose OK.

6. Click **C**lose on the Header and Footer toolbar.

Note: If you create a new document and insert a header to display on page two of the document, the header text may seem to disappear. The text is not lost, but will display when the document text is two pages in length. You may want to insert headers and footers when you finish typing the document.

Note: Be sure to use the Align Right button on the Formatting toolbar to position the header in formation rather than using the preset tabs. This eliminates possible header and/or margin problems.

PRACTICE

1. Open the file named *practice-42b*.

2. Create a right-aligned header in APA style to appear on every page. It will consist of a short version of the title followed by the page number.

History of the Internet (Click the Insert Page Number button.)

3. Click the Format Page Number button to start page numbering at page 2. Press ENTER after the page number is inserted in the header.

(continued on next page)

4. Click the Page Setup button on the Header and Footer toolbar to select Different first **p**age.

5. Click OK.

Your screen should look like this:

Remember to click the Page Number button instead of typing the page number in the header.

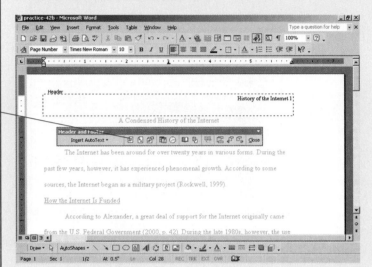

6. Close the Header and Footer toolbar.

7. Print your document. It should look similar to the following:

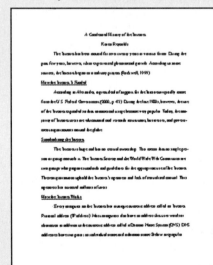

8. Save the file with the file name *student-42b*.

9. Return to GDP.

Go To
Textbook

Report Citations

Hanging Indent

To format a hanging indent:

1. Position the insertion point where you want to begin indenting (or select the text you want indented).
2. On the menu, choose F**o**rmat, **P**aragraph.
3. Select the indents and spacing tab if it is not already active.
4. In the **S**pecial box, click the down arrow and select Hanging; then choose OK.

    Or: On the keyboard, press CTRL+T.

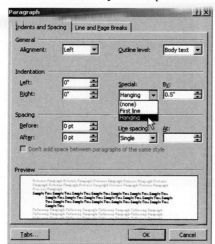

5. Type the paragraph. The first line begins at the margin. At the end of a line, text automatically wraps to the next line at the indent.
6. When you finish typing the hanging-indented text, press ENTER. Then, on the menu, choose F**o**rmat, **P**aragraph, **I**ndents and Spacing. In the **S**pecial box, click the down arrow and select (none). Then choose OK.

    Or: On the keyboard, press CTRL+SHIFT+T to return the insertion point to the left margin for all lines.

(continued on next page)

Note the changes that appear on the ruler when you format a paragraph with a hanging indent.

Hanging-indented passage

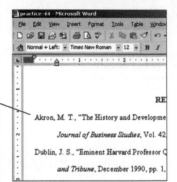

PRACTICE

1. Open the file named *practice-44*.
2. Select the two reference citations and format them with a hanging indent.
3. Position the insertion point at the end of the document, add this third reference citation, and format it with a hanging indent.

```
Veryl, L. J., Post, D. L., Edie, L., Lunt,
A. J., & Siegel, E. Y. First-Class Writing: A
Guide to English Usage and Misusage. Atlanta,
Georgia: Falcon Press, 1995.
```

(continued on next page)

4. Print the document. It should look similar to the following printout.

Note: Hanging indent material will either be single or double spaced depending on the type of reference style used. See the reference manual located in the front of your textbook or manual for details.

Two reference styles with hanging indents.

5. Save the document as *student-44*.

6. Return to GDP.

Lesson 45

Preliminary Report Pages

Tab Set—Dot Leaders

Word has default tab stops every 0.5 inch from the left margin. These are the tab settings you have been using to indent paragraphs. Word also enables you to set custom tabs at different positions and to fill the space before a tab stop with a row of periods (called dot leaders) to help lead the reader's eye across the page.

To set a custom tab using the menu:

1. Position the insertion point on the line where you want the new tab to start (or select the paragraphs where you want to change the tabs).
2. On the menu, choose Format, Tabs.
   The Tabs dialog box appears.

Type the position of each Tab stop position.

Select the Alignment.

Select Leader Option 2.

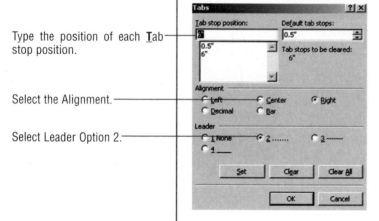

3. In the Tab stop position box, type the position of the tab you want to set.
4. In the Alignment box, select the desired alignment. (You would typically set a right tab for dot leaders.)
5. In the Leader box, select Option 2.
6. Choose Set.

Note: You can change from a dot-leader tab to hyphens or an underline by selecting Options 3 or 4.

7. Click OK.

Note: When you set a custom tab, default tabs to the left of the new setting will be deleted.

(continued on next page)

PRACTICE

1. Open a new document.
2. Set a left tab at 0.5
   Set a right dot-leader tab at 6 inches.
3. Type the following display:

```
President ...............................Brian Tuouy
Vice President ..........................Mary Mason
Secretary ...........................Timothy Kopacka
Treasurer .......................Janice Voyles-Nance
```

4. Save your file with the file name *student-45*.
5. Return to GDP.

Lesson 50

Letters in Modified-Block Style

Ruler Tabs

You can use the horizontal ruler to set tab stops and indents for selected paragraphs.

To display (or hide) the ruler:

On the menu, choose, **V**iew, **R**uler. The menu command will have a check mark beside it when the ruler is displayed. Be sure your ruler is displayed.

Tab Set

Word enables you to set left tabs, centered tabs, right tabs, and decimal tabs at different positions. Default tabs are displayed on the ruler as tick marks. Custom tabs are displayed according to type.

The four different kinds of tabs are illustrated below:

Tab Alignment button —

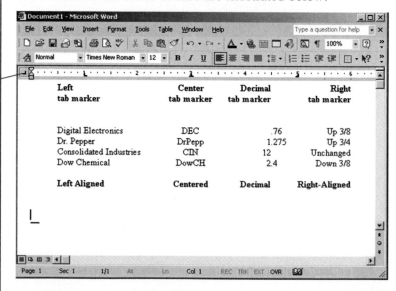

(continued on next page)

When you set a custom tab, Word clears (deletes) all of the default tab stops to the left of your custom tab. This allows you to go directly to the new tab stop when you press TAB.

To set a custom tab using the ruler:

1. Position the insertion point on the line where you want the new tab to start (or select the paragraphs where you want to change the tabs).

Left-aligned tab

Center tab

Right-aligned tab

Decimal tab

2. Click the Tab Alignment button on the ruler until the appropriate tab marker is displayed *(see illustration at left)*.
3. On the ruler, click where you want the new tab to appear.

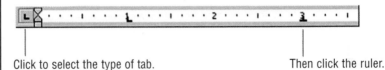

Click to select the type of tab.   Then click the ruler.

To clear or move a tab:

1. Position the insertion point on the line where you want the tab change to take effect (or select the paragraphs where you want to change the tabs).
2. To clear (delete) a tab, drag the tab marker off the ruler. To move a tab, drag the tab marker left or right.

PRACTICE

1. Open a new document.
2. Set a left tab at 1 inch on the ruler, a centered tab at 3 inches, and a right tab at 5 inches.
3. Type the following table; don't forget to press TAB before typing each item.

```
Eastern        Janie Baker            9,760
Central        Lanying Zhao          10,134
Western        J. Thomas Weisman      8,250
Caribbean      Felipe Menez             875
```

(continued on next page)

Your screen should look similar to the following:

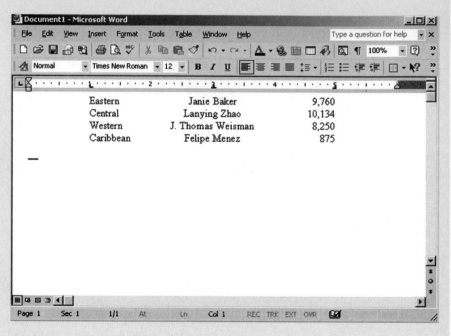

Eastern	Janie Baker	9,760
Central	Lanying Zhao	10,134
Western	J. Thomas Weisman	8,250
Caribbean	Felipe Menez	875

4. Save your file with the file name *student-50*.

5. Return to GDP.

Go To
Textbook

Traditional Resumes

Fonts

The term *font* refers to the general shape of a character. The default font in Word is Times New Roman. There are two types of fonts – serif and sans serif. A serif font has decorative lines. A sans serif font has no decorative lines. Shown below are some examples of different fonts you can use.

Times New Roman and Arial are available in any Windows document.

Serif fonts
Times New Roman
Palatino
Century Schoolbook

Sans Serif fonts
Arial Narrow
Helvetica
Tahoma

You can easily change the font in your text. Avoid, however, using too many different fonts in the same document.

To change fonts:

1. Position the insertion point where you want to begin using the new font (or select the text you want to change).
2. On the Formatting toolbar, click the down arrow to the right of the Font box.

Font box

(continued on next page)

3. Choose the font you want (scroll the list if necessary).

> **Or:** On the menu, choose F**o**rmat, **F**ont.

> **Or:** On the keyboard, press CTRL+D.

Select the Fo**n**t tab if it is not already active. When the Font dialog box appears, choose the font you want; then choose OK.

You can also change fonts (as well as other text attributes) through the Font dialog box.

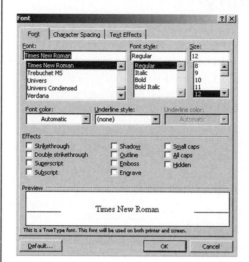

PRACTICE

1. Open a new document.

2. Center and type the following lines using the fonts indicated:

Courier New

Times New Roman

Arial

Brittanic Bold

3. Save your file with the file name *student-51*.

(continued on next page)

Table—Change Column Width

There are several ways to change table column width. In an earlier lesson, you learned the AutoFit to Contents feature. This lesson will show you how to change the column width using the mouse and the Table menu.

To change table column width using the mouse:

Mouse pointer

1. Point to the right border of the table column and when the mouse pointer turns into a vertical double bar with arrowheads, drag the column border to the desired width.

Note: As long as the cell is not selected, dragging the right border adjusts the entire column width, not just the cell width. Hold down ALT as you drag to see the exact ruler measurements. Double click the right border of a column to adjust the width of the column to the widest cell entry.

To change table column width using the menu:

1. Select the column or position the insertion point in the column. The insertion point will be bordered by an arrow on either side.
2. Choose Table P̲roperties from the T̲able menu.
3. Click the Col̲umn tab in the Table Properties dialog box.
4. Check Preferred w̲idth, if necessary, and key the value in the text box.
5. Click OK.

PRACTICE

1. Open the file named *practice-51*.
2. Point to the right border of the first column, press ALT, and drag the border to size the column to two inches.
   Note: As you drag the border to the left, an inch readout appears in the ruler window to let you know the width of the column.
3. Select the second column.
4. From the menu, choose T̲able, Table P̲roperties.
5. Select the Col̲umn tab if necessary.
6. Change the Preferred w̲idth to three inches.
7. Select the T̲able tab and choose C̲enter alignment
7. Choose OK.
8. Save the file with the file name *student-51b*.
9. Return to GDP.

Go To
Textbook

Electronic Resumes

Saving in Text-Only Format

A file format is the way information is saved and is indicated by a three-letter extension. The default extension for Word 2002 is *.doc*.

To save a document with a different file format:

1. Open the document you want to save using a different file format.
2. On the menu, choose **F**ile, Save **A**s.
3. The Save As dialog box displays.

If necessary, select the drive where you want to save the document.

4. Type a name for the document in the File **n**ame text box.
5. Choose the Text Only file format in the Save as **t**ype text box.

Choose a file format for the document.

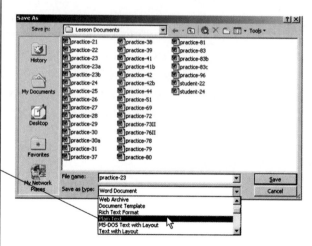

6. Click **S**ave.

PRACTICE

1. Open the file named *practice-23*.
2. Choose the Save **A**s command from the **F**ile menu.
3. Save this file with the new file name *student-52* and with the Plain Text file format.

(continued on next page)

4. Click **S**ave.

5. Click OK if a File Conversion dialog box appears.

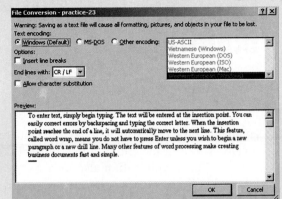

Go To
Textbook

6. Return to GDP.

Agendas and Minutes of Meetings

Hyphenation

Hyphenation reduces the ragged appearance of unjustified text because it divides words at the end of a line rather than moving the entire word to the next line. Hyphenation also reduces the amount of blank space inserted between words and letters in justified text.

To hyphenate words automatically:

1. From the menu, choose **T**ools, **L**anguage, **H**yphenation.
2. If it is not already selected, select the **A**utomatically hyphenate document check box.

   Note: When you access Word through the GDP software, the hyphenation feature is already turned on.

Select the **A**utomatically hyphenate document check box.

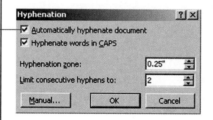

3. Set the number of consecutive hyphens at two.
4. Choose OK.

The hyphens Word inserts in words are called *soft hyphens* because they are used only when needed. If, during editing, a hyphenated word moves to the middle of the line, Word automatically removes the hyphen.

You can insert an optional (soft) hyphen in a word manually (for example, in a long proper name that is not in Word's dictionary).

To insert an optional hyphen:

1. Position the insertion point where you want to insert the optional hyphen.
2. Press CTRL+HYPHEN.

(continued on next page)

PRACTICE

1. Open a new file, and make sure the check box next to **A**utomatically hyphenate document is not checked.
2. Type the following paragraph, and print it.

   ```
   Another consideration to remember if you want to
   become a part of the emerging telecommunications field
   is that you must act professionally. Administrators
   receptive to innovative ideas proposed by their
   employees keep up with technology. Avoid embarrassment
   by ensuring that you are consistently prepared.
   ```

3. Turn on automatic hyphenation and print your document again. Compare the two printouts.
4. Save the file with the file name *student-67*.
5. Return to GDP.

Reports Formatted in Columns

Columns

You can prepare a document in newspaper-style columns or add columns to any part of your document. Text flows from the bottom of one column to the top of the next column. You must be in Print Layout View in order to view the columns on the screen.

To add columns to a document:

1. In Print Layout View, position the insertion point where you want the columns to begin, and select the text to appear in columns.
2. On the menu, choose Format, Columns. The Columns dialog box appears.

Text flows from the bottom of one column to the top of the next.

Type the number of columns desired.

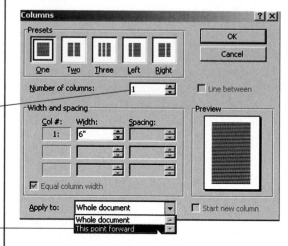

Select This point forward if you want the columns to begin at the insertion point.

3. Click on the correct Presets box or type the number of columns desired in the Number of columns box. If you want the columns to apply to the whole document, select Whole document in the Apply to area; if you want the columns to begin at the insertion point, select This point forward.
4. Choose OK.

(continued on next page)

As you're typing, when you reach the bottom of one column, the insertion point automatically moves to the top of the next column. Sometimes, however, you may want to force a column to break at a certain point. Or, you may want to have the text distributed equally among the columns to balance the text across the page.

To insert a column break:

1. Position the insertion point where you want to start the new column.

2. Press CTRL + SHIFT + ENTER.

To balance the columns:

1. Position the insertion point at the end of the text you want to balance.

2. On the menu, choose <u>I</u>nsert, <u>B</u>reak. The Break dialog box appears.

Balanced columns

Select Con<u>t</u>inuous to distribute the text evenly among all the columns.

3. Select Con<u>t</u>inuous; then choose OK.

The text is then evenly divided among all the columns.

PRACTICE

1. Open the file named *practice-69*.

WHAT TIME IS IT?

As human beings, our perception of time has grown out of a natural series of rhythms which are linked to daily, monthly, and yearly cycles. No matter how much we live by our wristwatches, our bodies and our lives will always be somewhat influenced by an internal clock. What is of even greater interest, though, are the many uses and perceptions of time based on individuals and their cultures.

Rhythm and tempo are ways we relate to time and are discerning features of a culture. In some cultures, people move very slowly; in others, moving quickly is the norm. Mixing the two types may create feelings of discomfort. People may have trouble relating to each other because they are not in synchrony. To be synchronized is to subtly move in union with another person; it is vital to a strong and lengthy partnership.

(continued on next page)

2. Select the second paragraph and format it in two columns.
3. Select the third paragraph and format it in three columns.
4. Position the insertion point at the end of the third paragraph and balance the columns. Your screen should now look like this:

WHAT TIME IS IT?

As human beings, our perception of time has grown out of a natural series of rhythms which are linked to daily, monthly, and yearly cycles. No matter how much we live by our wristwatches, our bodies and our lives will always be somewhat influenced by an internal clock. What is of even greater interest, though, are the many uses and perceptions of time based on individuals and their cultures.

Rhythm and tempo are ways we relate to time and are discerning features of a culture. In some cultures, people move very slowly; in others, moving quickly is the norm. Mixing the two types may create feelings of discomfort. People may have trouble relating to each other because they are not in synchrony. To be synchronized is to subtly move in union with another person; it is vital to a strong and lengthy partnership.

In general, Americans move at a fast tempo, although there are regional departures. In meetings, Americans tend to be impatient and want to "get down to business" right away. They have been taught that it is best to come to the point quickly and avoid vagueness. Because American business operates in a short time frame, prompt results are often of more interest than the building of long-term relationships.

---

5. Save the file with the file name *student-69*.
6. Return to GDP.

Go To Textbook

Special Letter Features

Sort

You can rearrange paragraphs or rows in a column by sorting them alphabetically, numerically, or by date.

To perform a sort:

1. Select the paragraphs to sort, or position the insertion point within the table. In this example, you would select the bulleted list.

Memory Specifications

- System clock
- Data rate
- Bandwidth
- Bus width

2. On the menu, choose T**a**ble, **S**ort. The Sort Text dialog box appears.

This list will be sorted alphabetically.

3. Under **S**ort by, choose paragraphs or the column that you want to sort, the type of sort (text, number, or date), and the sort order (ascending—low to high, or descending—high to low). For this sort, choose **P**aragraphs, **T**ext, **A**scending.

Note: If the column has a column heading you don't want included in the sort, under My list has, select Header **r**ow.

(continued on next page)

To undo a sort, click the Undo Typing button or choose **E**dit, **U**ndo, Typing.

4. Choose OK. The list is sorted as directed.

Memory Specifications

- Bandwidth
- Bus width
- Data rate
- System clock

PRACTICE

1. Open the file named *practice-72*.

> **VIDEO TERMINOLOGY**
> Chroma
> Motion Effects
> Overlay
> Frame Rate
> Compositing
> CODEC
> Aliasing
> Titling
> SMPTE Time Code
> Keyframe Animation
> Dropped Frame Rate

2. Sort the list alphabetically in ascending order. (Do not select the title.) Your screen should now look like this:

> **VIDEO TERMINOLOGY**
> Aliasing
> Chroma
> CODEC
> Compositing
> Dropped Frame Rate
> Frame Rate
> Keyframe Animation
> Motion Effects
> Overlay
> SMPTE Time Code
> Titling

3. Save the file with the file name *student-72*.

4. Return to GDP.

Go To
Textbook

More Special Letter Features

Shading

To give your table a more finished look, you can add shading.

To add shading:

1. Select the cells to which you want to add shading.
2. From the menu, choose F**o**rmat, **B**orders and Shading.
3. Select the **S**hading tab.

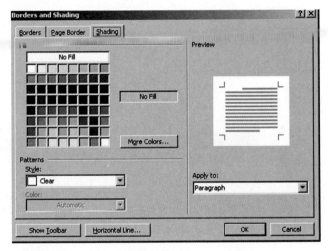

Shading Color button

Or: Click the Shading Color button on the Tables and Borders toolbar.

4. Select the shading option you want by clicking on the arrow in the Patterns, St**y**le box. "Clear" (the default setting) provides no shading. "Solid (100%)" provides a solid black shading, with the text appearing in white. A 10% or 20% shading provides a light gray shading, with the black text still visible.
5. Choose OK.

(continued on next page)

Solid (100%) shading ──

20% shading ──

Clear (no shading) ──

SALE		
Software Program	**Sale**	**Discount**
All-in-One	$439	37%
Corner Suite	295	40%
Suite Success	235	53%
InfoPro	189	46%
Friday	159	46%

PRACTICE

1. Open the file named *practice-73*.
2. Select the first row (containing the title and subtitle).
3. From the menu, choose F**o**rmat, **B**orders and Shading. Select the **S**hading tab, and apply a 100% shading to the first row (black).
4. Apply 20% shading to Row 2 (column titles) and Row 7 (TOTAL).

Your screen should now look like this:

SERVICE DEPARTMENT PAYROLL Week Ending June 7, 20--			
Employee	**Hours**	**Rate**	**Gross Pay**
Luis J. Bachman	40.00	$ 8.93	$ 357.20
Austin Engerrand	18.25	7.80	142.35
Louise W. Vik	35.50	13.45	477.47
Robert Wendlinger	37.75	16.50	622.88
TOTAL			$1,599.90

5. Save the file with the file name *student-73*.
6. Return to GDP.

Go To
Textbook

Multipage Memos With Tables

Find and Replace

Use Find to search for text in a document. Use Replace to both search for text and replace the found text with revised text. For example, if you misspell JoAnn's name as "Jo Anne," you could replace all occurrences of the name in one step.

To find text (without automatically changing it):

1. From the menu, choose **E**dit, **F**ind.

  Or: From the keyboard, press CTRL+F.

  The Find and Replace dialog box appears with the Fin**d** tab active.

Type the text you want to find. ———

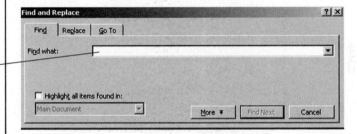

  Note: Click **M**ore to expand the dialog box and display other options. Or, if the box is already expanded, click **L**ess to shrink the box.

2. Type the text you want to find in the Fi**n**d what text box.

3. Choose **F**ind Next.

  If Word finds the text, it highlights that text in the document. You can edit the text without closing the Find dialog box and then continue the search by choosing **F**ind Next again.

4. To close the dialog box, choose Cancel or press ESC.

To replace text:

1. From the menu, choose **E**dit, R**e**place.

  Or: From the keyboard, press CTRL+H.

  The Find and Replace dialog box appears with the Re**p**lace tab active.

(continued on next page)

Type the original (incorrect) text in the Fi**n**d what text box and the new (corrected) text in the Replace wi**t**h text box.

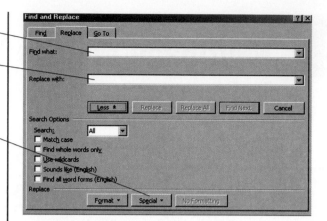

Select F**o**rmat or Sp**e**cial to search for and/or replace non-printing characters (such as a tab character or a font change).

Note: Click **M**ore to expand the dialog box and display other options. Or, if the box is already expanded, click **L**ess to shrink the box.

2. Type the text you want to replace in the Fi**n**d what text box.

3. Press TAB and type the text you want to replace it with in the Replace wi**t**h text box.

4. Choose **F**ind Next.

   If Word finds the text, it highlights it in the document. To replace the text, choose **R**eplace; to leave it unchanged, choose **F**ind Next.

   Note: To automatically change all occurrences of the text in the document without the program stopping to ask you to verify each change, choose Replace **A**ll.

5. When Word finishes, Close in the Find and Replace dialog box.

Hands On

PRACTICE

1. Open the file named *practice-42b*.

2. Use R**e**place to find all occurrences of "users" and replace it with "subscribers."

   Note: You should have located and changed two occurrences.

3. Save the file with the file name *student-74*.

4. Return to GDP.

Go To
Textbook

Tables with Footnotes or Source Notes

Table—Text Direction

The default orientation for text in a table is horizontal. Sometimes, however, you may want to format the text in a table to display vertically.

To change the text direction or orientation of text in a table:

1. Click the cell that contains the text to be changed.

2. On the menu, choose Format, Text Direction.

Change Text Direction button.

Or: Click the Change Text Direction button on the Tables and Borders toolbar.

Vertically Top-to-Bottom

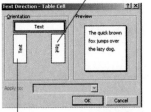

3. Select the text direction for vertically top-to-bottom or vertically bottom-to-top.

4. Drag down on the bottom border of the row with the vertical text until the text displays in one continuous line without wrapping.

5. Click OK.

Note: Text rotates in 90-degree increments.

Vertically
Bottom-to-Top

Hands On

PRACTICE

1. Open a new document.

2. Insert a boxed table with 4 columns and 5 rows, and type the table below, merging the cells in Row 5.

Northern Departures	Interior Stateroom	Ocean View Stateroom	Additional Guest
5/24	$699	$799	$299
6/31	799	899	350
7/7	899	999	400
Note: Dates may vary.			

3. Do not change the left alignment of the column headings.

4. Right-align the text in the number columns.

5. Select Row 1 and change the text direction to display vertically top-to-bottom.

(continued on next page)

6. Drag down on the bottom border of Row 1 until the column headings display in one continuous line without wrapping.

7. Click in the table and apply the Auto**F**it to Contents feature.

8. Center the table horizontally and vertically.

	Northern Departures	Interior Stateroom	Ocean View Stateroom	Additional Guest
5/24	$699	$799	$299
6/31	799	899	350
7/7	899	999	400
Note: Dates may vary.			

Table Resize Handle

9. Save the file with the file name *student-76a*.

Table—Insert or Delete Rows or Columns

Before you can insert or delete rows or columns, you must first select the row or column. Word inserts a new row above the selected row and a new column to the *left* of the selected column.

Note: The Insert Table button on the Tables and Borders toolbar and the **I**nsert option on the T**a**ble menu provide options for choosing whether rows are inserted above or below and whether columns are inserted to the left or to the right of selected text.

To insert a row:

1. Position the insertion point outside the table to the left of the row you want to select; then click. The selected row is highlighted.

Click to the left of the row you want to select.

Software Program	List	Sale	Discount
All-In-One	$695	$439	37%
Corner Suite	$495	$295	40%
Suite Success	$495	$235	53%
InfoPro	$350	$189	46%
Friday	$295	$159	46%

(continued on next page)

2. With the row still selected, click the right mouse button to open the Shortcut menu; then choose **I**nsert Rows.

Choose **I**nsert Rows from the Shortcut menu.

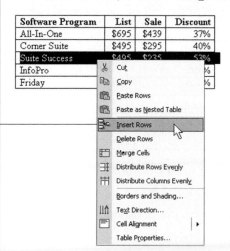

A new blank row appears above the selected row.

Software Program	List	Sale	Discount
All-In-One	$695	$439	37%
Corner Suite	$495	$295	40%
Suite Success	$495	$235	53%
InfoPro	$350	$189	46%
Friday	$295	$159	46%

To insert a column:

1. Point to the top border of the column you want to select. When the insertion point changes to a solid arrow, click. The selected column is highlighted.

Point to the top border of the column you want to select.

Software Program	List	Sale	Discount
All-In-One	$695	$439	37%
Corner Suite	$495	$295	40%
Suite Success	$495	$235	53%
InfoPro	$350	$189	46%
Friday	$295	$159	46%

To insert a new row at the end of a table, position your insertion point in the last cell (the last 46% in this case) and press TAB.

(continued on next page)

2. With the column still selected, click the right mouse button to open the Shortcut menu; then choose **I**nsert Columns. A new blank column appears to the left of the selected column.

Software Program	List		Sale	Discount
All-In-One	$695		$439	37%
Corner Suite	$495		$295	40%
Suite Success	$495		$235	53%
InfoPro	$350		$189	46%
Friday	$295		$159	46%

To delete a row or column:

1. Select the row or column.

2. Click the right mouse button to open the Shortcut menu.

3. Choose **D**elete Rows or **D**elete Columns.

PRACTICE

1. Open the file named *practice-76*.

2. Select and then delete the column labeled "List."

3. Insert a new row immediately above the Row 5 (the InfoPro row).

4. Type the following information in the new Row 5:
   Perfect Star   230   39%

Your table should now look like this:

Software Program	Sale	Discount
All-In-One	$439	37%
Corner Suite	$295	40%
Suite Success	$235	53%
Perfect Star	$230	39%
InfoPro	$189	46%
Friday	$159	46%

5. Save the file with the file name *student-76b*.

6. Return to GDP.

Lesson 78

Tables Formatted Sideways

Page Orientation

The default page orientation for 8 1/2- × 11-inch paper is vertical (also called *portrait*). Sometimes, however, it is more convenient to format a page in horizontal orientation (called *landscape*).

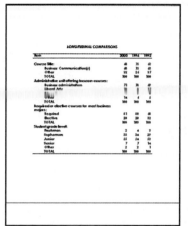

Portrait Orientation

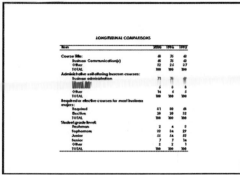

Landscape Orientation

To change the page orientation:

1. On the menu, choose **F**ile, Page Set**u**p.

2. Select the **M**argins tab.

Select either Portra**i**t (vertical) or Lands**c**ape (horizontal) orientation.

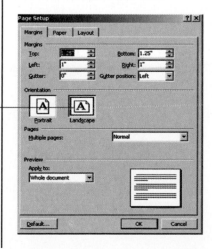

(continued on next page)

3. In the Orientation box, select either **P**ortrait (vertical) or Landscape (horizontal).

4. Choose OK.

PRACTICE

1. Open the file named *practice-78*.
2. Move the insertion point to the beginning of the document.
3. Change the page orientation to landscape.
4. Switch to Print Pre**v**iew. Your document should look like this:

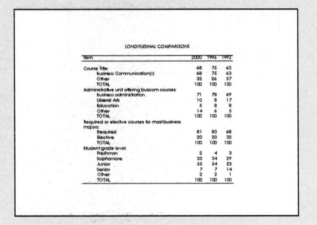

5. Save the file with the file name *student-78*.
6. Return to GDP.

Lesson 79

Multipage Tables

Repeating Table Heading Rows

The second page of most multipage tables will not make sense to the reader if the column headings are not repeated on each page. Consider, for example, the following two-page table:

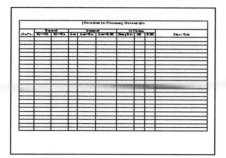 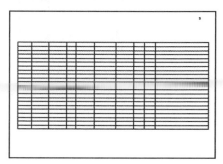

Without headings, page 2 is just a series of empty cells.

To repeat a table heading on subsequent pages:

1. Select the rows of text (including the first row) that you want to use as a table heading.

Worksheet for Processing Manuscripts									
	Rejected		Accepted			In Process			
Ms. No.	RJ—Ed	RJ—Rev	Acc	Acc—Rev	Acc—R&R	Being Rev	AR	R&R	Short Title

2. From the menu, choose Ta**b**le, **H**eading Rows Repeat.
   The headings are now repeated on each page.

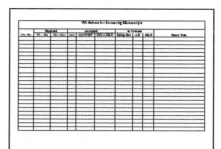 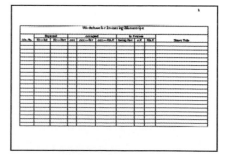

(continued on next page)

PRACTICE

1. Open the file named *practice-79*, which contains a two-page table.

2. Select the first three rows of the table, and click the **H**eading Rows Repeat option on the T**a**ble menu.

3. Print page 2 of the table. It should look like the following illustration.

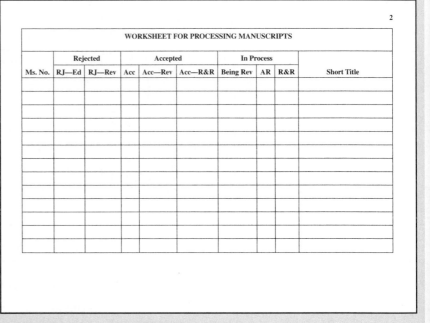

4. Save the table with the file name *student-79*.

5. Return to GDP.

Using Predesigned Table Formats

Table—AutoFormat

Word has several features that automatically change formatting. One of these features is Table AutoFormat.

To automatically format a table:

1. Click the table.

	Northeast	Southeast	Northwest	Southwest
1002	$436,789	$246,890	$369,135	$275,678
2004	$598,034	$354,035	$410,239	$356,871
2006	$673,090	$491,444	$555,397	$478,231

Table AutoFormat button

2. From the menu, choose T**a**ble, Table Auto**F**ormat.

Or: Click the Table AutoFormat button on the Tables and Borders toolbar.

3. Choose a format from the **T**able Styles box. Scroll if necessary.

4. Apply special formats.

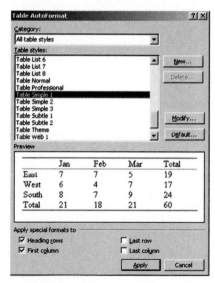

5. Click Apply.

(continued on next page)

PRACTICE

1. Open the file named *practice-80*.
2. Click the table, and choose the Table Auto**F**ormat option on the T**a**ble menu.
3. Choose the Table Contemporary.
4. Click Apply.
5. Save the table with the file name *student-80*.
6. Return to GDP.

Formal Report Project

Styles

A *style* is a collection of formatting commands that has been assigned a name and saved. You might, for example, want to create a style named "Center" to center a report heading in all caps and in bold, followed by a blank line. You can then easily apply all of the formatting commands to the text in one step. Later, if you modify the style, all of the text to which that style has been assigned will automatically reflect the changes.

Every paragraph in a Word document has a paragraph style applied to it. The default style is called the *Normal* style.

Normal

The Normal style displayed in the Style box on the Formatting toolbar.

To create a new style:

1. From the menu, choose F**o**rmat, **S**tyles and Formatting Click New Style.

2. Choose New Style. The New Style dialog box appears.

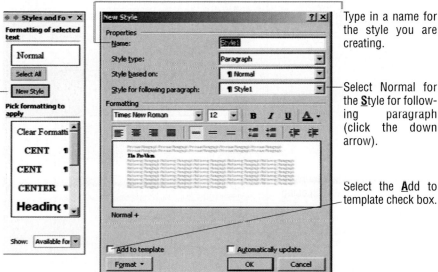

Click New Style

Type in a name for the style you are creating.

Select Normal for the **S**tyle for following paragraph (click the down arrow).

Select the **A**dd to template check box.

3. Type a descriptive name for the new style in the **N**ame text box.

4. Click the down arrow in the **S**tyle for following paragraph box and select Normal.

5. Check the **A**dd to template check box if you would like the style to be available for all of your documents. *(continued on next page)*

6. Click the F**o**rmat button and choose **F**ont. Choose formatting options for the style. For example, in the Center style, you would select Bold and **A**ll caps. Then choose OK.

Select Bold and **A**ll caps.

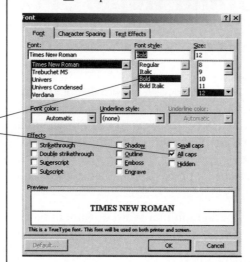

7. In the New Style dialog box, click the F**o**rmat button again and choose **P**aragraph. Be sure the **I**ndents and Spacing tab is active; then choose the formatting options. For the Center style, go to Ali**g**nment and select Centered. Then go to Spacing, Aft**e**r and select 12 pt (which leaves 1 blank line after). Then choose OK.

Select Centered in the Ali**g**nment box and 12 pt in the Spacing Aft**e**r box.

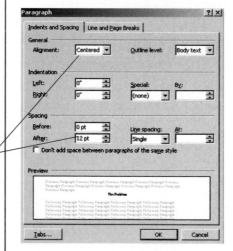

8. Choose OK to define the style. Close the Styles and Formatting Task Pane.

Note: To delete a style you no longer need, choose **F**ormat, **S**tyle. Then select the unwanted style and choose Delete.

(continued on next page)

To apply a style:

1. Position the insertion point where you want the style formatting to take effect or select the text to which you want to apply a style.

Select the text to which you want to apply a style.

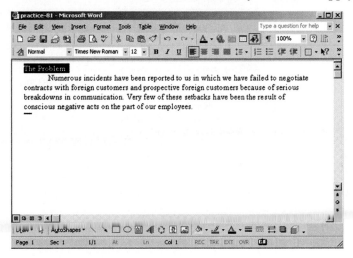

2. In the Style box on the Formatting toolbar, click the down arrow; then choose the style you want to apply.

Choose the style you want to apply.

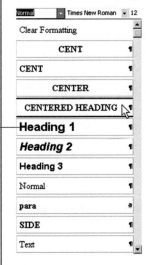

Selected (highlighted) text will take on the formatting characteristics of the applied style, or any new text you type will be formatted according to the style.

Note: If you are applying a style to new text, when you press ENTER you will return to the Normal style.

(continued on next page)

Note: To apply a border to any side of a blank line, follow the steps in Lesson 37, Tables—Borders. However, position your insertion point on the desired line on a page rather than inside.

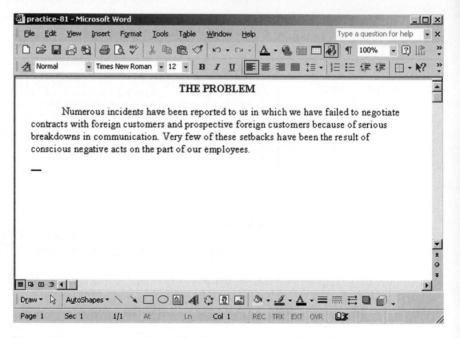

Note: To remove a style applied in error, select the affected text and apply the Normal style (or click Undo).

PRACTICE

1. Open the file named *practice-81*.
2. Create a style named "Centered Heading" that will center a report heading in all caps and bold, followed by a blank line.
3. Apply the style "Centered Heading" to the report heading labeled *The Problem.* Your screen should now look like the one shown above.
4. Save the file with the file name *student-81*.
5. Return to GDP.

Format Report Project

Insert Clip Art and Files

One of the easiest ways to make a document interesting is to add a graphic or picture. Pictures can be sized easily and positioned within a document.

Many different graphics (clip art images) are available to you in Word. You may also use other available clip art images as long as they are compatible with Word. Additional clip art information can be found at www.gdp.glencoe.com.

To add a picture to a document:

Drawing button

1. Display the Drawing toolbar by clicking the Drawing button on the Standard toolbar.

Drawing toolbar

2. Or: From the menu, choose <u>V</u>iew, <u>T</u>oolbars, Drawing.

3. Click the Insert Clip Art button on the Drawing toolbar.

Insert Clip Art button

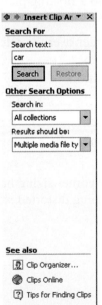

(continued on next page)

4. Or: From the menu, Choose **I**nsert, **P**icture **C**lip Art.

5. In the Insert Clip Art task pane, in the Search text box, type a word or phrase describing the type of clip you want.

6. Click Search.

7. Scroll by clicking the arrow to select the clip you want.
Note: To clear the search and start with another category, click Modify.

8. In the Results box, click the clip you want to insert it.

To find more Clip Art Online:

Clips Online button

1. Click Clips Online from the bottom of the Task Pane window.

2. Enter your network password to connect to the Web.

3. Click the image of your choice or conduct a search for additional Clip Art.

To position the picture:

1. Select the picture by clicking it. The Picture toolbar displays. If necessary, right-click on the selected picture and choose Show Picture Toolbar.

Text Wrapping button

2. Click the Text Wrapping button and choose **S**quare.

Note: By default pictures are inserted as an **I**n line with text picture. To change an in line picture to a floating picture, you must select a wrapping style.

4-Headed arrow for moving

3. Position the mouse pointer over the selected graphic until it changes to a 4-headed pointer.

4. Drag the graphic to position.

To size the picture:

1. Select the picture by clicking it. The Picture toolbar displays.

2. Position the mouse pointer over a sizing handle until the pointer turns into a 2-headed arrow.

2-Headed arrow for sizing

Note: Use one of the four-corner sizing handles to resize a picture to prevent the picture from being distorted when it is resized.

(continued on next page)

3. Drag the sizing handle and notice that a dotted-line box appears. The box represents the new size. Release the mouse button.

A selected picture has sizing handles.

Drag one of the top or bottom sizing handles to adjust the height.

Drag one of the middle sizing handles to adjust the width.

Drag one of the corner sizing handles to adjust the width and height and to maintain the original proportions.

Format Picture button.

Note: A second way to size a picture is to select the picture and to click the Format Picture button on the Picture toolbar.

4. Click the Size tab and change the height and width values.

5. Click OK.

Hands
On

PRACTICE

1. Open the file named *practice-83*.

2. Insert a picture at the top of the document.

3. Change the wrap style to square.

4. Size the picture to be approximately 1 inch wide.

5. Drag the picture to horizontally center the picture in the second paragraph.

(continued on next page)

Your document should look similar to this:

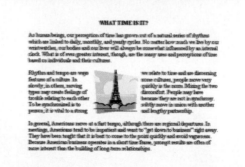

6. Save the file with the file name *student-83a*.

INSERT A FILE

There may be times when you want to combine two Word documents. To insert a Word document into the current active document:

1. Position the insertion point.
2. On the menu, choose **I**nsert, Fi**l**e.
    The Insert File dialog box displays.

Click here to display the contents of a different drive.

If the folder or file you want to open is displayed, double-click to open it.

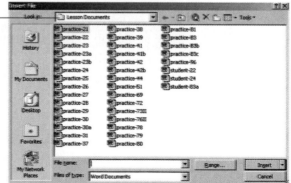

3. Choose the correct folder in the Look **i**n box. A list of files is displayed.
4. Double click the file name to insert the document at the insertion point.

(continued on next page)

Hands On

PRACTICE

1. Open the file named *practice-83c*.

2. Position the insertion point below the picture.

3. On the menu, choose <u>I</u>nsert, Fi<u>l</u>e.

4. Locate the file *practice-83b*.

5. Double click the file name.

Your document should look similar to this:

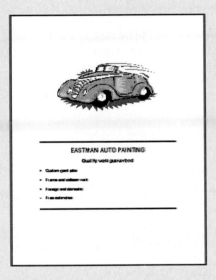

6. Save the file with the file name *student-83b*.

7. Return to GDP.

Go To
Textbook

International Formatting (Canada)

Paper Size

The default paper size is the standard 8.5 × 11 inches. You can, however, change the paper size if your printer has the capability of handling different-sized paper.

To change the paper size:

1. From the menu, choose File, Page Setup.

2. Select the Paper tab.

3. Click the down arrow under Paper size, and select the paper size desired.

A4 metric paper size has been selected.

Page Setup [?][X]

| Margins | Paper | Layout |

Paper size:
[A4 ▼]

Width: [8.27"] [↕]

Height: [11.69"] [↕]

Paper source

First page:
Default tray (Automatically S ▲
Automatically Select
Auto Select
Upper Paper Tray
Manual Paper Feed
Lower Paper Tray ▼

Other pages:
Default tray (Automatically S ▲
Automatically Select
Auto Select
Upper Paper Tray
Manual Paper Feed
Lower Paper Tray ▼

Preview

Apply to:
[Whole document ▼]

[Print Options...]

[Default...]   [OK] [Cancel]

4. To select a custom size of paper (for example, half-page size, or 5.5 × 8.5 inches), click the down arrow under Paper size, then scroll down and select Custom size. Change the Width and Height to the appropriate sizes.

(continued on next page)

Type in the desired paper dimensions.

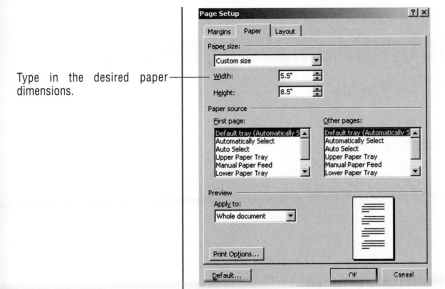

5. Choose OK.

PRACTICE

1. Open the file named *practice-86*.

2. Change the paper size to A4.

3. Add an envelope to the document and choose the DL envelope size option.

4. Save the file with the file name *student-86*.

5. Return to GDP.

International Formatting (Mexico)

Insert Symbol

Many foreign languages include diacritical marks or a combination of characters to indicate phonetic sounds. The Symbol dialog box contains many of the characters needed to type words with special accents.

To insert a symbol:

1. Position the insertion point where you want to insert a symbol or select an existing letter.

2. On the menu, choose **I**nsert, **S**ymbol, **S**ymbols tab.

An international character can by inserted by using a shortcut key. Microsoft Word Help provides a list of symbols and shortcut keys.

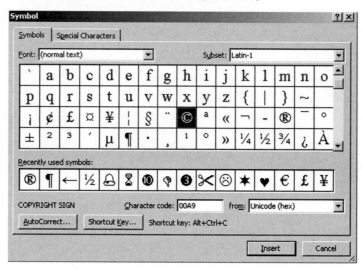

3. Select (normal text) in the **F**ont box.

4. Click a symbol to see a highlighted view.

5. Click **I**nsert to insert the symbol and click Close.

6. Check the capitalization of the symbol. It may be necessary to change from uppercase to lowercase.

(continued on next page)

PRACTICE

1. Open a new file and insert a table with four columns and six rows.
2. Type the following information in the table. Be sure to insert the appropriate symbol as shown above selected letters in the Spanish and French columns.

English	Spanish	English	French
Wednesday	Miércoles	telephone	le téléphone
little girl	niña	Christmas	LeNoël
bus	autobús	student	l' élève
airplane	avión	French	le français
birthday	cumpleaños	window	le fenêtre

3. Apply the Auto<u>F</u>it to Contents feature.
4. Center the table horizontally and vertically.
5. Select the first row and format the text with bold, small caps, and center alignment.
6. Change the row height of the first row to .4 and vertically align the text in the center of each cell. Your table should now look like this:

English	Spanish	English	French
Wednesday	Miércoles	telephone	le téléphone
little girl	niña	Christmas	LeNoël
bus	autobús	student	l' élève
airplane	avión	French	le français
birthday	cumpleaños	window	le fenêtre

7. Save the file with the file name *student-87*.
8. Return to GDP.

Legal Office Applications

Line Numbering

To number lines in a document—for example, in legal documents—you can use Word's line numbering command. Line numbers can be positioned, formatted, and turned on or off as needed. Line numbers can also be restarted within a document.

Word will add line numbers to every line in the document unless you have divided your document into sections. In a legal document, line numbering should begin on the first line of the first paragraph. Therefore, a section break must be inserted at this point in the document.

To insert a section break to begin a new section at the first paragraph:

Click the Show/Hide ¶ button on the Standard toolbar so you can see the section break.

1. Position the insertion point at the beginning of the paragraph.

2. On the menu, choose **I**nsert, **B**reak. The Break dialog box appears.

3. Select Con**t**inuous in the Section break types area and choose OK.

To begin line numbering:

1. Position the insertion point at the start of the paragraph where you want line numbering to begin.

2. Switch to Print Layout View and then choose Page Width view from the Zoom drop-down list on the Standard toolbar so that you will be able to see the line numbering in the space between the left edge of the page and the left margin.

(continued on next page)

3. On the menu, choose **F**ile, Page Set**u**p. The Page Setup dialog box appears.

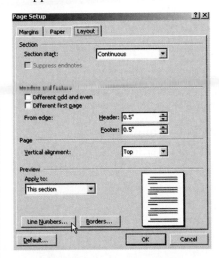

4. Select the Layout tab, and click the Line **N**umbers button. The Line Numbers dialog box appears.

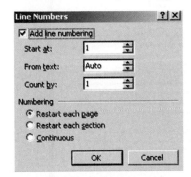

5. Check the Add **l**ine numbering box.

Note: The rest of the default settings are already correct for standard line numbering.

(continued on next page)

6. Choose OK to exit the Line Numbers dialog box, and choose OK to exit Page Setup and begin line numbering at the insertion point.

PRACTICE

1. Open the file named *practice-96*.

2. Switch to Print Layout View and Page Width view.

3. Click the Show/Hide ¶ button, place the insertion point at the beginning of the first paragraph **before** the tab; then choose Continuous from the Section break types.

Move the insertion point here, before the tab, to insert a section break before numbering the lines.

4. Turn on line numbering.

5. Position the insertion point at the first blank line before the signature lines and choose Continuous from the Section break types.

6. Turn off line numbering.

7. Save the file with the file name *student-96*. Your document should now look like this.

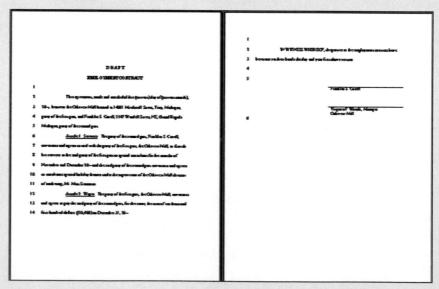

Go To
Textbook

8. Return to GDP.

Lesson 101

Using Correspondence Templates

CorrespondenceTemplates

Every document that you create is based on a template, which defines margins, tab settings, toolbars displayed, and additional formatting. When you start Word and begin typing in the document window, you are using Word's default template, called the "Normal" template.

Instead of using this normal template, you can create a document by opening any one of Word's predefined document templates. You might want to use one of Word's correspondence templates such as a memo or letter template.

Note: Microsoft does not always include the same templates when it upgrades Word. If you do not have a required template in your current installation of Word, please refer to the Glencoe keyboarding Web site at www.gdp.glencoe.com for information regarding the location of needed templates.

To use a memo template:

1. Choose **F**ile, **N**ew from the menu. The New Document task pane appears.
2. Select General Templates. The new dialog box appears.

Note: To use a template other than the default template, you must access the New command from the menu—rather than using the toolbar or the keyboard.

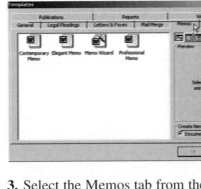

Select the appropriate tab for the type of document you wish to create.

Ensure that **D**ocument is selected in the Create New box.

3. Select the Memos tab from the new dialog box.
4. Select the first memo template listed in your word processing software.

(continued on next page)

Note: To use a letter template, click the Letters & Faxes tab; then select the desired letter template.

3. Choose OK. The predefined document appears.

Note: Word will default to Print Layout View.

Word assigns a temporary file name until you save your document.

Click to select the text in brackets, and replace it with your own data. Delete any unwanted text.

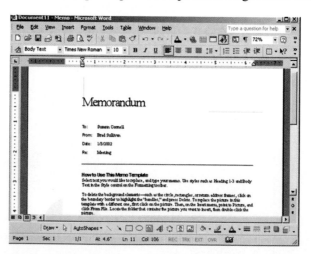

4. Click to select the text in brackets and type your replacement text.

Note: If you are replacing a single-line entry with a multiple-line entry, press SHIFT + ENTER between lines to avoid inserting extra space between the lines.

5. Select and delete any parts of the template text you don't need (such as the copy notation).

The bracketed text has been replaced by appropriate text.

The Body Text style of this template automatically inserts extra space between paragraphs. Therefore, press ENTER only once between paragraphs.

6. Follow the instructions on the template to make other changes.

After completing this template, it might look like the following:

7. Save the document as you normally would.

(continued on next page)

PRACTICE

1. Open a new document and use the first memo template.

2. Type a memo from you to `Helen Lalin` on the subject of "`Luncheon Invitation`." Use the current date and send a copy to `Jose Limon`.

3. Delete the confidential notation. (Move to the bottom of the page and select the text frame. Click the frame to select and press delete. Open the Footer pane, click on the rectangle object to select it and press delete.)

4. Type the body of the memo.

Notes:

- The first line of the memo template instruction is an H1 style. Delete the first line of text. The remaining paragraphs are the body text style. Select the text and begin typing without pressing DELETE

- If you delete the text, you may delete the paragraph style and embedded formatting.

- When you press ENTER 1 time at the end of the first paragraph, Word adds an extra line, which is the blank line between the two paragraphs.

The message of this short memo is as follows:

```
I will be happy to attend the luncheon meeting of the
Purchasing Managers' Association with you next Tuesday
at the Friar's Club. Since I'll be at a workshop until
11:15 that morning, I'll meet you in the lobby of the
Friar's Club at 12:15 p.m.

 Thanks for thinking of me.
```

Your screen should look similar to the following:

5. Save the file with the file name *student*-101.

6. Return to GDP.

Go To

Textbook

Using Report Templates

Report Templates

Word's standard templates are accessed by clicking <u>N</u>ew on the <u>F</u>ile menu. When the New dialog box opens, you will see templates listed by category.

Note: Microsoft does not always include the same templates when it upgrades Word. If you do not have a required template in your current installation of Word, please refer to the Glencoe keyboarding Web site at www.gdp.glencoe.com for information regarding locating the templates you need.

To use the contemporary report template:

1. Click <u>F</u>ile; then click <u>N</u>ew to display the New document task pane.
2. Click General Templates to open the New templates dialog box.
3. Click the Reports tab to display the Reports templates available in Word.
4. Select the first template; then click OK. The first Reports template contains four text placeholders. If necessary, click the Show/Hide button on the toolbar to display the paragraph marks attached to each placeholder.
5. Drag to select the text in the text placeholders. Be careful not to delete the paragraph marks since they contain formatting instructions.
6. Type the replacement text and notice that each placeholder is formatted with a style. You can apply a different style to text in a template and delete sample text placeholders.
7. Save the document.

(continued on next page)

PRACTICE

1. Open a new document and use the first report template.

2. Select the text in the "Type Address Here" placeholder and type the following:

```
4066 Main Avenue
Orlando, Florida 32806
```

3. Drag to select the company name "blue sky associates" and type `Digital Media`.

4. Drag to select the text title "FilmWatch Division Marketing Plan" and type `New Technologies`.

5. Drag to select the text subtitle "Trey's Best Opportunity . . . " and press delete.

(continued on next page)

Your screen should look similar to the following:

Digital Media

New Technologies

6. Save the unfinished report with the file name *student-102*.

7. Return to GDP.

Go To
Textbook

Designing Letterheads

Small Caps

You can vary the appearance of text by changing the font to small caps. The first column below illustrates words typed in all caps, initial caps, and lowercase. The second column illustrates the same text typed in small caps.

Normal	Small Caps
ALL CAPS	ALL CAPS
Initial Caps	INITIAL CAPS
lowercase	LOWERCASE

To create small caps:

1. Position the insertion point where you want to begin using small caps (or select the text you want to change).
2. On the menu, choose Fo**r**mat, **F**ont, and be sure the Fo**n**t tab is active.
   Or: On the keyboard, press CTRL+D.
3. When the Font dialog box appears, select S**m**all caps; then choose OK.

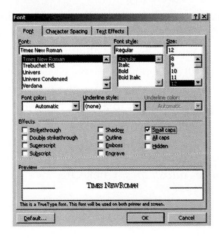

(continued on next page)

PRACTICE

1. Open a new file.
2. Click the Tab Alignment button on the ruler until the left tab marker is displayed and click the 1-inch mark on the ruler.
3. Type the following memo heading using small caps formatting instead of all caps for the heading information.

   To: Garland Peters
   From: Leigh Rogers
   Date: Current Date
   Subject: Vacation Leave

4. Save your file with the file name *student-103*.

Text Boxes

A text box can be used to insert and emphasize text (for example, an important quote). Text inside the box can be formatted, the borders and fill can be changed, and the box can be positioned and sized freely.

To add a text box to a document:

1. Switch to Print Layout View and then choose Whole Page view from the Zoom drop-down list on the Standard toolbar to position the text box more efficiently.

Drawing button

2. On the Standard toolbar, click the Drawing button to display the Drawing toolbar on the bottom of the screen.
3. On the Drawing toolbar, click the Text Box button. A drawing canvas appears on your page.

Text Box button

Cross hair pointer

4. To create the text box, move the mouse pointer inside the document (the pointer changes to a cross hair). Position the cross hair where you want the text box to appear; then drag to create the text box.

   Note: To remove the drawing canvas, click Tools, **O**ptions and then the General tab. Uncheck *automatically create drawing canvas when inserting Autoshapes*. Click OK.

(continued on next page)

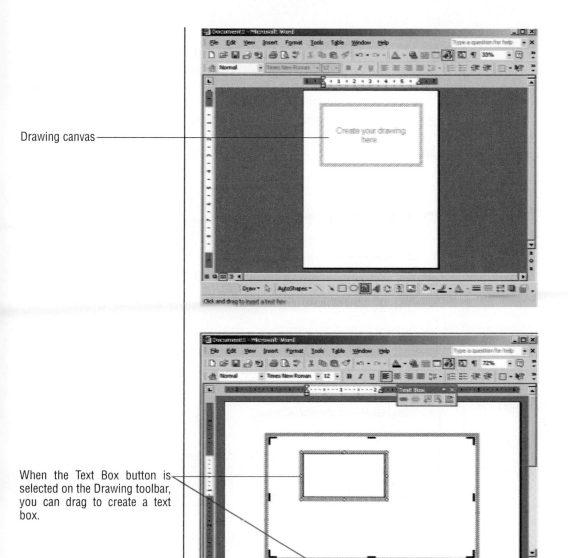

Drawing canvas

When the Text Box button is selected on the Drawing toolbar, you can drag to create a text box.

Drawing toolbar

A shaded outline of the box will appear.

5. Switch to **P**age width view. Click within a text box to activate it. Format and type any text; then click outside the text box when you are finished.

Note: If the text does not fit within the box, you must manually resize the box.

(continued on next page)

To position and size the text box:

1. Switch to Whole Page view; then click the text box border to select the text box. Notice the difference between the appearance of the text box border when you select the border versus the appearance of the text box border when you click within a text box.

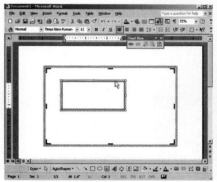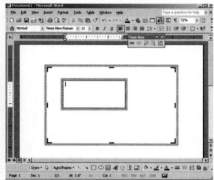

Selecting the text box border   Clicking in the text box

2. Position the mouse pointer on one of the outer edges of the text box until the pointer changes to a 4-headed positioning pointer.

    Note: Sizing handles will appear on the edges of the text box when it has been selected.

Positioning pointer

If you lose sight of your textbox, use **P**age width and **W**hole page view to see the box.

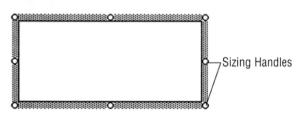

Drag one of the top or bottom sizing handles to adjust the height.

Sizing Handles Drag one of the middle sizing handles to adjust the width.

Drag one of the corner sizing handles to adjust the width and height in one step.

3. Drag the text box to position it. (An outline of the box will appear as you drag it.)

    Note: Once a text box is selected, you can also use the directional arrows or CTRL+ directional arrows to position the box.

4. Position the mouse pointer on a sizing handle until the pointer changes to a 2-headed pointer; then drag to size the box. Repeat this step for all sides of the box.

2-headed pointer

(continued on next page)

Line Style button

Line Color button

Fill Color button

Font Color button

To change the borders in a text box:

1. Select the text box.
2. On the Drawing toolbar, click the Line Style button and click the desired line style.
3. On the Drawing toolbar, click the down arrow next to the Line Color button and click the desired line color.

To change the fill in a text box:

1. Select the text box.
2. On the Drawing toolbar, click the Fill Color button and click the desired color.

To edit the text in a text box when the insertion point is no longer inside the text box:

1. Click in the box to select it, and begin editing the text.

   Note: You may change the Font or Font Color as desired.

2. When you are finished editing text, click outside the box to exit the text box.

PRACTICE

1. Open the file named *practice-103*.
2. Create a text box in the area indicated below.

```
                                    ─────Insert a text box in this area.




        Sun Industries
        799 Wilshire Boulevard
        Los Angeles, CA 90017
```

3. Change to Arial Regular 28 point, press ENTER once, and center and type `Benefits Plan` inside the text box.
4. Add borders using a 4 1/2-point line, and apply a Gray-25% fill.

   Note: To apply a border to any side of a blank line, follow the steps in Lesson 37, Tables—Borders. However, position your insertion point on the desired line on a page rather than inside a table.

(continued on next page)

5. Size the new text box so the text inside the box is vertically centered.

6. Save the file with the file name *student-103*. Your finished document should look something like this:

Go To
Textbook

7. Return to GDP.

Designing Notepads

Print Options

When you click the Print button on the Standard toolbar, the entire document will print. If you choose **P**rint from the **F**ile menu, you can select print options. You can choose to print on a specified number of pages or to a specified paper size.

To define print options:

1. On the menu, choose **F**ile, **P**rint. The Print dialog box displays.

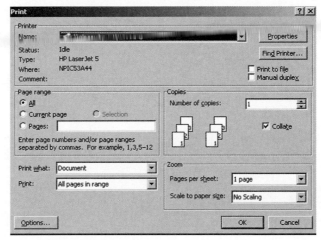

Note: Changes to print options are not saved for future printing.

2. Click the down arrow to open the Pages per s**h**eet drop-down list. Choose the number of pages to print per sheet of paper.

3. Click the down arrow to open the Scale to paper si**z**e drop-down list. Choose the scaling option.

(continued on next page)

PRACTICE

1. Open the file named *practice-42b*.
2. Open the Print dialog box and choose 4 pages per sheet in the Zoom section.
3. Choose the A4 paper size in the Scale to paper size drop-down list.
4. Click OK.
5. Close the document.
6. Return to GDP.

Designing Cover Pages

Word Art

WordArt is a drawing tool used to create special effects with text. A WordArt object can be formatted, rotated, realigned, and stretched to predefined shapes. The color and fill of the WordArt object can also be changed.

To insert a WordArt object:

1. Display the Drawing toolbar.

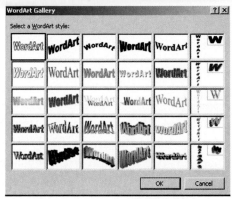

2. Click the Insert WordArt button on the Drawing toolbar.

3. Choose a style from the WordArt Gallery dialog box.

Insert WordArt button

4. Click OK.

5. Type your text in the Edit WordArt Text dialog box.

6. Choose <u>F</u>ont and <u>S</u>ize for the text.

(continued on next page)

7. Click OK.

The WordArt object is inserted in the document and the WordArt toolbar displays.

WordArt Gallery button

Format WordArt button

WordArt Shape button

To format a WordArt object:
1. Select the WordArt object if necessary.
2. Click the WordArt Gallery button to change the <u>W</u>ordArt style.
3. Click the Format WordArt button on the WordArt toolbar.
4. Select the Colors and Lines tab to change the Fill and Line colors.
5. Select the Size tab to change the H<u>e</u>ight and Wi<u>d</u>th of the WordArt object.
6. Select the Layout tab to change Wrapping style and Horizontal alignment.
7. Click the WordArt Shape button to change the shape of the WordArt object.

PRACTICE

1. Open a new file and display the Drawing toolbar.
2. Click the Insert WordArt button.
3. Choose a style from the WordArt Gallery dialog box and click OK.
4. Type `Gaston Consulting` and choose a font.
5. Click OK.
6. Click the Format WordArt button, and select the Colors and Lines tab.

   Or: Click the WordArt toolbar.
7. Change the Fill and Line colors and click OK.

(continued on next page)

Your screen should look similar to this:

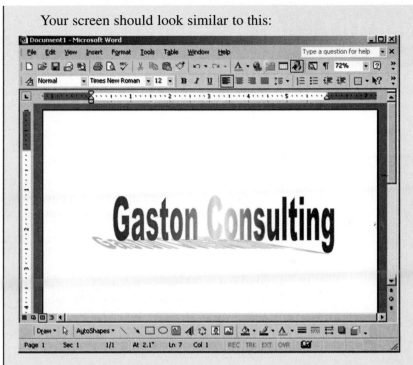

8. Save the file with file name *student-106*.

9. Return to GDP.

Go To

Textbook

Lesson 107

Designing Announcements and Flyers

Table—Move

The Table **Pr**operties dialog box contains options for table alignment. The options for aligning a table include left, right, and center alignment. You can also choose a value to indent the table from the left margin.

If you want to position a table at a specific location on the page, use the move table feature.

Table Move Handle

Mouse pointer positioned on top of Table Move Handle.

To move a table:

1. Place the mouse pointer on the table until the Table Move Handle appears.
2. Point to the Table Move Handle until a four-headed arrow appears.
3. Drag the table to the new location.

   Note: Switch to Print Layout View or reduce the **Z**oom level if necessary for a better view of the table position on the page.

PRACTICE

1. Open the file named *practice-107* and format the document using landscape orientation.
2. Move the mouse pointer over the table.
3. Point to the Table Move Handle and drag the table to the center of the page.

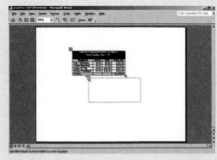

(continued on next page)

4. Switch to Print Pre_v_iew. Your document should look like this:

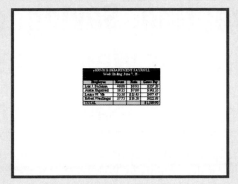

5. Save the file with the file name *student-107*.
6. Return to GDP.

Creating, Saving, and Viewing Web Pages

Web Page—Saving and Viewing

By default Word saves documents with the .doc extension. Word can also save documents as Web pages by converting them to HTML (HyperText Markup Language) file format. Files saved using HTML format can be displayed in a Web browser such as Microsoft Internet Explorer.

When a file is saved as a Web page, several things happen:

Note that Web Page (*.htm; *.html) is indicated as the file format.

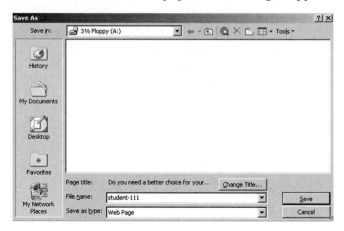

New Web Page button

 Web Layout

Web Layout View button

- On the Standard toolbar, the New Blank Document button changes to the New Web Page button.

- The document view changes to Web Layout View. Text wraps to fit the window size rather than the margins, and objects are positioned as they would be in a Web browser.

To save a document and convert it to HTML format:

1. From the menu, choose **F**ile, Save as Web Pa**g**e.

2. In the Save As dialog box, click the down arrow next to the Save **i**n box; if necessary, browse to the drive and directory where you want to save the Web page.

(continued on next page)

3. In the File **n**ame box, type a file name for the Web page.

Note: In the Save as **t**ype box, the file name extension changes from .doc to .htm. Do not type the period or the *htm* extension.

4. Click the **S**ave button.

PRACTICE

Note: Practice Exercises Lessons 111, 112, 114, and 115 are designed to Create, Save and View Web Pages (with Hyperlinks). It is important to perform Practice Exercises in sequential order. Do not skip or change the sequence of Lessons 111 through 115.

1. Open the file named *practice-111*.

2. Note the New Blank Document button on the Standard toolbar, note the Print Layout View button next to the horizontal scroll bars, and note the text wrapping in the first line. You will compare your observations in this step to Step 4.

3. Save the file as a Web page named *student-111*. Remember that the extension (.htm) is automatically added for you.

4. Observe these changes: on the Standard toolbar, the New Blank Document button was replaced by the New Web Page button; the Web Layout View button next to the horizontal scroll bars is active; and the text wrapping in the first line has changed.

5. Close the file named *student-111*.

Tables provide the framework and infrastructure for many Web page designs. By placing text inside a table, you can exercise some control over line endings when the page is displayed in a Web browser. You can also insert pictures inside the cells in a table to control their positions. Empty rows are often used in the layout of a Web page to visually separate table information.

Do you need a better choice for your digital phone service? DigitalCom can offer you two free services. Please browse around our site for details.

Web Layout View ——————

Call Waiting	Call Forwarding
• Take a second call without ending your current call.	• Receive calls no matter where you are.
• A special tone alerts you that someone is calling.	• Forwards all your calls to a designated phone.

(continued on next page)

Web Layout View is used to design a Web page. If you have created any open tables, gridlines will be visible. However, to view your page as it will look in a Web browser, use the We**b** Page Preview feature. In We**b** Page Preview, table gridlines are not visible and line endings may vary from those in Web Layout View. The size and resolution of the monitor and the Web browser being used cause line endings to change.

We**b** Page Preview (Browser View)

Do you need a better choice for your digital phone service? DigitalCom can offer you two free services. Please browse around our site for details.

Call Waiting
- Take a second call without ending your current call.
- A special tone alerts you that someone is calling.

Call Forwarding
- Receive calls no matter where you are.
- Forwards all your calls to a designated phone.

To preview a document as a Web page in a browser:

1. From the menu, choose **F**ile, We**b** Page Preview.
2. Word opens your default browser and displays your document as a Web page.

Note: You do not have to have an Internet connection to use We**b** Page Preview, but you must have Web browser software installed.

3. Click the **C**lose button in your browser window to close it.

PRACTICE

1. Open the file named *practice-111a*.
2. Insert an empty row above Row 2 ("Call Waiting") to visually separate the introductory paragraph from the column headings. You will have to merge the two cells of the table.
3. Insert a row with 2 columns below the last row in the table.
4. Type this sentence as the second bulleted item under the heading `Call Waiting`: `A special tone alerts you that someone is calling.`
5. Type this sentence as the second bulleted item under the heading `Call Forwarding`: `Forwards all your calls to a designated phone.`
6. Save the file as a Web page named *student-111a*.

(continued on next page)

7. Note that table gridlines are visible. Also note the line endings in the first row of the table. You will compare your observations in this step with Step 8.

8. View the Web page in a browser. Note that your table gridlines are not visible and note any changes in your line endings.

9. Close your browser, and close your document.

10. Return to GDP.

Lesson 112 Creating Frames

Web Page—Frames

Frames are used to divide a Web page into sections. When a new frame is added above a Web page, the Web page is split into two separate horizontal sections. The top section is called the header frame and the bottom section is called the main frame.

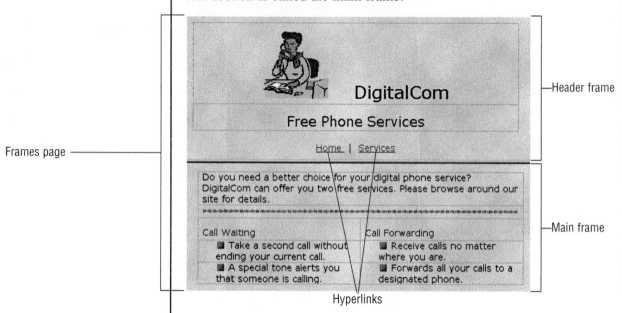

Frames page

Header frame

Main frame

Hyperlinks

A header frame is used to hold any information that should appear consistently at the top of every page in the Web site. Text, tables, pictures, hyperlinks, etc., may be inserted into the header frame. In a Web site with several pages, hyperlinks may be used in the header frame. As each hyperlink is clicked, a different page is displayed in the main frame below.

Because the frames page usually acts as the home or starting page in a Web site, you might have to save it using a specific name if you are going to publish the Web site. Some host servers require a file name such as *index.htm* or *index.html* in order for the Web site to be published and functional on their server computer.

(continued on next page)

When you save the frames page, the header frame is automatically assigned a name and saved at the same time. You, therefore, end up with three files: the main page you initially opened, which is now re-saved; the header frame page, which is automatically named and saved when you save the frames page; and the frames page itself, which displays both the header frame and the main frame simultaneously. It is often easier to open the frames page rather than the header frame page or the main page to edit the pages of the Web site.

To add a header frame and create a frames page:

1. Open an existing main page.

2. On the menu, choose, Format, Frames, **N**ew Frames Page.

Frames toolbar

Note: The Frames toolbar displays automatically. You may need to drag the title bar to reposition the toolbar.

3. From the Frames toolbar, click the New Fra**me** Above button. Your screen will be split into a blank header frame and a main frame

4. Type the desired information into the header frame, preferably within a table. If you need to delete an incorrect frame, click inside the frame to be deleted and click the Delete Frame button on the Frames toolbar.

Note: If you use tables, remember to center them horizontally.

5. Position your mouse pointer over the frame border until the pointer becomes a double-headed arrow.

6. Drag the frame border below the header frame until the header frame is the desired size.

7. Save the frames page with the desired file name.

Hands
On

PRACTICE

Note: Practice Exercises Lessons 111, 112, 114, and 115 are designed to Create, Save and View Web Pages (with hyperlinks). It is important to perform Practice Exercises in sequential order. Do not skip or change the sequence of Lessons 111 through 115.

1. Open the file named *practice_main-112*.
   Note: This file is the main page of the Web site.

(continued on next page)

Note: Any document in which *main* is used as part of the file name is a main page in a Web. Any document in which *index* is used as a part of the file name is a frames page.

Frame border

2. Center the table horizontally.
3. Add a header frame.

Header frame

Main frame

Do you need a better choice for your digital phone service? DigitalCom can offer you two free services. Please browse around our site for details.

Call Waiting	Call Forwarding
• Take a second call without ending your current call.	• Receive calls no matter where you are.
• A special tone alerts you that someone is calling.	• Forwards all your calls to a designated phone.

4. Click inside the header frame, and create an open table with 2 rows.
5. Center the table horizontally.
6. In Row 1, center and type `DigitalCom`.
7. In Row 2, center and type `Free Phone Services`.
8. Size the header frame to minimize scrolling.
9. Save the document as a frames page named *student_index-112*.

Frames page

DigitalCom
Free Phone Services

Do you need a better choice for your digital phone service? DigitalCom can offer you two free services. Please browse around our site for details.

Call Waiting	Call Forwarding
• Take a second call without ending your current call.	• Receive calls no matter where you are.
• A special tone alerts you that someone is calling.	• Forwards all your calls to a designated phone.

(At this point, a simple Web infrastructure of 3 files is created: a header frame file is automatically created, named, and saved *DigitalC*; the original *practice_main-112* file is re-saved and overwritten; and a frames page is created, named *student_index-112*.)

10. View the Web page in a browser, close the browser, and close the file.
11. Return to GDP.

Go To
Textbook

Creating Web Pages with Hyperlinks

Web Page—Hyperlinks

A hyperlink is an object (usually text or a picture) you click to jump from one place to another. You might use a hyperlink to move within a Web page, to move to another Web page or Web site, or perhaps to open a different software program.

To create a text hyperlink on a Web page:

Insert Hyperlink button

1. Open the frames page.
2. Select the text for the hyperlink.
3. From the Standard toolbar, click the Insert Hyperlink button. The Insert Hyperlink dialog box appears.

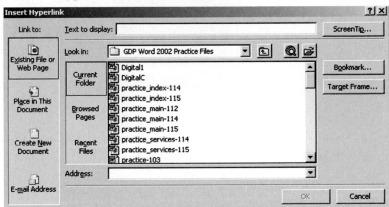

4. If necessary, under Link to on the left, click Existing File or Web Page to link to an existing file or Web page.
5. Under Browse for on the right, click the File button and browse to locate the file. If necessary, change the Files of type to Office Files.
6. Click the desired file name.
7. Click Target Frame. Click the frame where you want the linked document to appear. In this case, click the bottom section, which represents the main frame. The frame turns dark blue when selected.

(continued on next page)

Be sure the correct file name appears in this box or the hyperlink will point to the wrong page.

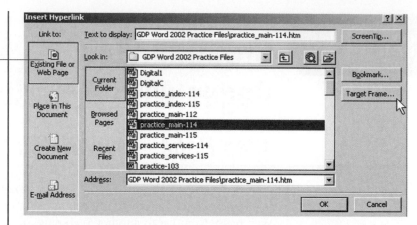

8. Click OK twice, and click the Save button to save the frames page.

Click this bottom frame so that the linked document will appear in this frame.

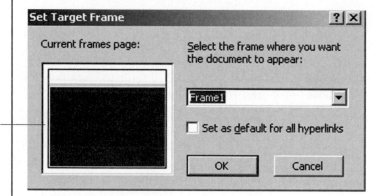

To test the hyperlinks:

1. With the frames page open, click each hyperlink.

   Note: If necessary, press CTRL while clicking to activate the hyperlink.

2. If the desired page appears in the main frame, the hyperlink is successful.

To remove or edit a hyperlink:

1. Right-click on the hyperlink.

2. From the shortcut menu, click **H**yperlink, then click **R**emove Hyperlink or Edit **H**yperlink and make the desired changes.

(continued on next page)

Hands
On

PRACTICE

Note: Practice Exercises Lessons 111, 112, 114, and 115 are designed to Create, Save and View Web Pages (with hyperlinks). It is important to perform Practice Exercises in sequential order. Do not skip or change the sequence of Lessons 111 through 115.

(If the words <u>Home</u> and <u>Services</u> do not appear in the bottom of the top frame when practice_index.114 is open, proceed with the following): Click the header frame in the first blank line below the table. Press ENTER 1 time and type Home followed by two spaces, the pipe symbol (|) followed by two spaces, and type Services.

1. Open the frames page file named *practice_ index-114*.

2. Assign a hyperlink to the word *Home* in the header frame to point to the corresponding Web page named *practice_main-114*.

3. Assign a hyperlink to the word *Services* in the header frame to point to the corresponding Web page named *practice_services-114*.

4. Save the Frames page as *student_index–114*, and test the hyperlink. (At this point, a simple Web infrastructure is created: a header frame file is automatically created, named, and saved *DigitalC*; the main page file, *practice_main-114,* is re-saved; and a frames page is created, named *student_index-114*.)

5. Edit any hyperlinks as needed, and save the frames page again.

6. View the Web pages in a browser, close the browser, and close the frames page.

7. Return to GDP.

Go To

Textbook

Formatting Web Pages

Web Page—Design Themes

A theme is a unified collection of design elements such as coordinated backgrounds, fonts, bullets, colors, and graphics. Applying a theme to the pages in a Web site transforms it instantly and provides unity and visual appeal. When you save the pages after applying a theme, several subfolders and files are automatically created and saved as a part of the Web site. They hold any graphics files used by the theme.

After you have applied a theme, you can also apply styles to selected lines on the page. Styles should be used to make titles and headings distinct and uniform. Themes and styles can be changed easily, so have fun and experiment.

To apply a theme:

1. Open the frames page.

2. Click in the header frame.

3. From the menu, choose F**o**rmat, T**h**eme.

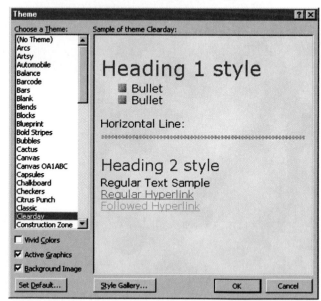

(continued on next page)

4. Click the name of a theme in the Choose a **T**heme list.

Note: A sample of the theme is displayed in the sample area. Click different themes to preview them.

5. Click OK to apply the desired theme.

Note: The theme's formatting will be instantly applied to the Web page, and the subfolders holding the theme's graphics will be automatically created.

6. Click on a hyperlink in the header frame to display a different page in the main frame.

7. Apply a theme as explained in Steps 3-5.

8. Continue opening all Web pages and applying the same theme to each until the desired theme has been applied to all pages.

9. Click the Save button to save changes to all pages.

To apply a style:

1. Select the desired text.

2. From the Formatting toolbar, click the down arrow next to the Style box; then click the desired style.

Style box

Available styles ────────

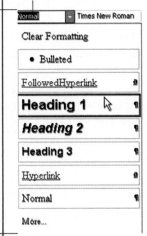

Note: You may need to re-size the frames so that all the information is visible without scrolling.

(continued on next page)

To change a theme:

1. Open the desired Web page.
2. From the menu, choose Format, Theme.
3. Click the name of the new theme in the Choose a Theme list.
4. Click OK to apply the desired theme.

PRACTICE

Note: Practice Exercises Lessons 111, 112, 114, and 115 are designed to Create, Save and View Web Pages (with hyperlinks). It is important to perform Practice Exercises in sequential order. Do not skip or change the sequence of Lessons 111 through 115.

1. Open the frames page file named *practice_ index-115*.
2. Apply a theme to the header frame.
3. Save this file as *student_index-115*.
4. Click the Services hyperlink to display the services page in the main frame, apply the same theme, and save *student_index-115* again. Click the Home hyperlink to display the home page in the main frame, apply the same theme, and save *student_115* again. Note: If necessary, press CTRL while clicking to activate the hyperlink.
5. Apply a heading style with the largest font to DigitalCom in the header frame so that the business name is outstanding. Center the line if needed.
6. Apply a heading style to Free Phone Services in the header frame so that the subtitle displays with a smaller font than the business name. Center the line if needed.
7. Apply a consistent style to the headings *Call Waiting*, *Call Forwarding*, *Setting Up Call Waiting*, and *Setting Up Call Forwarding* in the linked pages.
8. Click in one of the blank rows on the page displayed in the main frame.
9. On the Formatting toolbar, click the down arrow next to the Outside border button; then click the Horizontal Line button to insert a horizontal line in the blank row.

Outside Border button

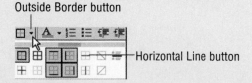

Horizontal Line button

(continued on next page)

10. Continue adding horizontal lines to all blank rows.

11. Change any font colors as desired.

12. Insert a picture in the header frame if desired.

    Note: You may need to re-size the picture.

13. View the Web pages in a browser, and then close the browser. Note: In the browser, you might need to click the Home and Services hyperlinks to display the frames page correctly.

14. Save student_index–115 again, close the files, and then return to GDP.

Appendix A

Start Word From Windows

To start Microsoft Word from Windows:

1. If you have not done so, turn on your computer and start Windows.
2. Locate the Microsoft Word application file. It might be identified by the file name "Winword.exe" or by any of these icons:

On some systems, this icon will be located in the Microsoft Office shortcut bar, which may be located at the top right of the desktop.

On any system, you can click the Start button, and then point to Programs to find the Microsoft Word application file.

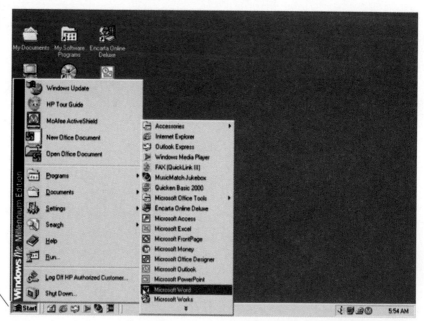

Click the Start button and point to Programs to find the Word icon.

3. If the Word icon is on the desktop, double-click to open Word. If it is in the Microsoft Windows shortcut bar or if you access it from the Start button, click once to open Word.

In a few seconds, Word displays its main screen with a blank document ready for your input. (If you see a Tip of the Day, read the tip; then click OK to close the tip callout.)

The appearance of the screen depends upon the defaults that have been set for your computer. It also depends upon what settings have been used in Word 2002. Dynamic toolbars change as features are used.

Title bar

Menu bar
Standard toolbar
Formatting toolbar

Insertion point

End-of-document marker

Mouse pointer

Scroll bars

Office Assistant

Status bar
Start button
Taskbar

4. The mouse pointer shows the location of the pointer on the screen. The pointer takes on different shapes, depending on where it is positioned on the screen and the task on which you are working. With your mouse, point to each of these items on your screen:

• *Title bar:* Displays the name of the application program you're running (Microsoft Word) and the name of the current document (until documents have been saved, Word identifies them as *Document1, Document2,* and so on).

• *Menu bar:* Displays the list of choices available.

• *Standard toolbar:* Displays buttons that you can click with the mouse to perform common tasks.

• *Formatting toolbar:* Displays information about formats and buttons you can click to change formats.

• *Ruler:* Shows the page margins, tabs, and indentions.

• *Insertion point:* Shows where text will appear when you type.

• *End-of-document marker:* Shows the position of the last character in your document.

- *Scroll bars:* Are used to display parts of the document that are not currently visible.
- *Status bar:* Displays information about your document and the position of the insertion point.
- *Start button:* Displays a menu that contains everything you need to begin using Windows.
- *Taskbar:* Contains a button representing each program and Word 2002 document that is open.

Quit Word

To quit Microsoft Word and return to the Windows Desktop:

1. On the title bar, click Word's close button at the far right.

   Note: Do not confuse the *Word* Close button on the title bar with the *document* Close button just below it on the menu bar. Clicking the document Close button would close the active document but would not quit Word.

   Or: On the keyboard, press ALT+F4.

   If you have not saved your document, Word prompts you to save it. You're then returned to the Windows Desktop.

Word Close button

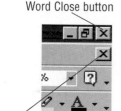

Document Close button

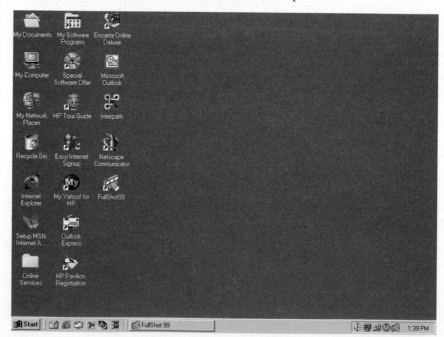

A Brief Introduction to the Internet

Overview—What is the Internet?

The Internet, also known as the Net, is a massive worldwide network of computers. Through the Internet, you can access information, conduct research, participate in discussion groups, play games, shop for just about anything, and send email to friends, businesses, and family. The Internet is a valuable source on any topic. You can look at newspapers from anywhere in the world, read magazines, get tax forms and information on how to complete them, and even search for a job. You can also learn about worldwide events almost as soon as they happen.

Even the most farsighted Internet pioneers did not predict the enormous growth and the tremendous impact the Net has had on global communication. Experts even have difficulty calculating how many millions of people use the Internet daily from either their homes or their workplaces.

The Internet started in 1969 when the Advanced Research Projects Agency (ARPA) of the United States Department of Defense connected computers at different universities and defense contractors. The goal of the ARPANET was to build a network with multiple paths that would survive a disaster and to provide computing resources to users in remote locations. ARPANET expanded rapidly, and in the mid '80s the National Science Foundation (NSF) created NSFnet to complement ARPANET. The link between ARPANET and NSFnet was the Internet. The Internet continued to grow as private companies developed their own networks and connected to the Internet through gateways. In 1990 the original ARPANET was discontinued. Today the Internet connects thousands of networks and million of users.

The Internet is huge and has no central ownership. This means that no single person or group controls it. The Internet Society and the World Wide Web Consortium are two groups who propose standards and guidelines for the appropriate use of the Internet. These organizations uphold the Internet's openness and lack of centralized control. This openness has attracted millions of users.

(continued on next page)

There are many ways to access the Internet including connecting through a LAN (local area network), modem, or high-speed data link. To connect a desktop computer to the Internet you need appropriate hardware (modem or network interface card) and software. An Internet Service Provider (ISP) provides Internet software, and there is a monthly fee for Internet services. Be sure to shop around for your ISP because there are a variety of plans available. Estimate how many hours you will be using the Internet and then choose a plan that suits your needs.

How the Internet Works

Every computer on the Internet has a unique numeric address called an Internet Protocol address (IP address). Most computers also have an address that uses words or characters in addition to the numeric address called a Domain Name System (DNS). DNS addresses have two parts consisting of an individual name and a domain name. The chart shows popular domain names used in the United States. Domain addresses outside the United States use country codes in the domain name. (Example: .fr for France)

Internet Domains		
Domain	**Type of Organization**	**Example**
.com	Business (commercial)	ibm.com (International Business Machines Corp.)
.edu	Educational	umich.edu (University of Michigan, Ann Arbor, MI)
.gov	Government	whitehouse.gov (The White House)
.mil	Military	navy.mil (The United States Navy)
.net	Gateway or host (or business/commercial)	mindspring.net (Mindspring, a regional Internet service provider)
.org	Other organization (typically nonprofit)	isoc.org (The Internet Society)

(continued on next page)

Internet Elements

The Internet has many elements and offers various services. Some of the most popular elements of the Internet include the World Wide Web, search engines, Web browsers, electronic mail (email), newsgroups, and FTP—File Transfer Protocol.

The World Wide Web (WWW) is a graphical system on the Internet. A Web site is a location where an individual, a university, a government agency, or a company stores Web pages. These Web pages contain information about a particular subject. A Web site is a collection of related Web pages. A *hit* is the term used to indicate that someone has viewed a Web page. Popularity is determined by how many hits a Web page has accumulated. By clicking on a graphic or picture in the Web site, you may jump to a different Web page through the use of Hypertext markup language (HTML). The hypertext links are the foundation of the World Wide Web.

Web browsers are used to find and view Web pages. You need to have a browser to access the World Wide Web and open the documents on your computer. Two of the most popular browsers are Microsoft Internet Explorer and Netscape Navigator. Web browsers gather resources from the Internet and put this information at your fingertips.

Electronic mail (email) is the most commonly used Internet tool. People are able to communicate with friends, family, and co-workers anywhere in the world. You can create an address book to record frequently used email addresses. You can send files as attachments with email messages. Sending emails is easy, instant, and inexpensive.

Newsgroups are electronic bulletin board services on the Internet. There are thousand of newsgroups, and each is dedicated to a discussion of a particular subject. Anyone may post an article about the newsgroups topic. You can read all the articles posted as well as see the initial entry that started the topic of discussion.

File Transfer Protocol (FTP) Internet tool is used to copy files from one computer to another. A good example of this type of use on the computer is at tax time. You are able to access a government Web site and download any information about taxes, including any forms you may need.

(continued on next page)

The Internet and You

In a short period of time, the Internet has become an integral part of school, home, and work. The Internet enhances our lives by offering new job opportunities, work-from-home offices, shopping for goods and services from anywhere (e-commerce), entertainment, and expanded research opportunities. It is an extraordinary communication tool. The Internet's reach and usefulness is limitless.